Sherry
and the Wines
of Spain

Plate 1. A bodega courtyard, Jerez
(*see* Chapter 2)
Kenneth Swain

Sherry
and the Wines
of Spain

George Rainbird

WITH COLOUR PHOTOGRAPHS BY KENNETH SWAIN,
PERCY HENNELL, AND THE AUTHOR
AND MAPS BY AUDREY FREW

McGRAW-HILL BOOK COMPANY

NEW YORK   TORONTO   LONDON   SYDNEY

Designed and produced for
McGraw-Hill Book Company
by George Rainbird Limited,
2 Hyde Park Place, London W2

The jacket, end-papers, and colour plates
were printed in the Netherlands
by L. van Leer and Company N.V.
of Amsterdam

The text and maps were printed,
and the binding carried out,
by Butler & Tanner Limited of Frome, Somerset, England

First printing
© George Rainbird Limited 1966

Library of Congress Catalog Card Number 66–25521

51152

CONTENTS

Page

ILLUSTRATIONS

COLOUR PLATES

LINE DRAWINGS

Acknowledgements

A book of this sort cannot be written without a great deal of help from a great number of people, and this I have received in full measure. The research required is formidable in itself, both at home and in Spain; I am afraid I have made a lot of busy people even busier in working out introductions and arranging for samples of wine from those distant parts of Spain to which I could not travel.

First, I wish to give my grateful thanks to the Dirección General de Expansión Comercial of the Ministerio de Comercio in Madrid, and particularly to its Sub-Director, Señor Don Miguel Angel Santamaría, who was able to use a very powerful magic on the other associated government departments in Spain; and, in London, my thanks with equal gratitude to the Commercial Office of the Spanish Embassy, where Señor Don Manuel Quintero and Señor Don Gabriel Ferrán have been unstinting in their efforts to facilitate my local and Spanish researches and to make available documents that have proved to be of the utmost service.

Representatives of the Spanish wine trade in England have all been most helpful, including and in particular Señor Don Alejandro Cassinello of La Riva, who, it seems, has important connections not only in Jerez, but throughout the length and breadth of the Iberian Peninsula, and Mr L. W. Steer, who is the Chairman of the Rioja Wine Shippers Association, and was able to make available, not only specialized information, but some very specialized wine that I had not known existed.

I am further indebted to:

Sr Don Antonio Alarcón, Alarcón Hermanos, S.A., Córdoba

Sr Don Francisco Rodríguez Alvárez, Secretario General, Sindicato Nacional de la Vid, Paseo del Prado, Madrid

Sr Don Alvaro de Alvear, Alvear, S.A., Montilla, Córdoba

Sr Don Juan Amigó, Amigó Hermanos y Cía, Reus, Tarragona

Sr Don P. Ankersmit, Scholtz Hermanos, S.A., Málaga

Sr Don Joaquín Arteaga, Bodegas Bilbainas, Valdepeñas, Ciudad Real

Sr Don José María Vidal Barraquer, Estación de Viticultura y Enología, Villafranca del Panadés, Barcelona

Sr Don José Antonio López Cascante, José López Bertrán y Cía, Tarragona

Cooperativa Alella Vinícola, Alella, Barcelona

Sr Don Marcelo Frias, Bodegas Riojanas, S.A., Cenicero, Logroño

Sr Don Cruz García Lafuente, Bodegas Las Veras, S.A., Fuenmayor, Logroño

Sr Don Gerardo Sánchez Gómez, Bodegas Morenito, Valdepeñas, Ciudad Real

Sr Don Pedro Lòpez de Heredia, R. López de Heredia, Viña Tondonia, S.A., Haro, Logroño

Sr Don Antonio Larrea, Consejo Regulador de la Denominación de Origen Rioja, Logroño

Bodegas Marqués de Murrieta, Ygay, Logroño

Bodegas Palacio, S.A., Laguardia, Alava

Sr Don José María Raventós, Codorníu, San Sadurní de Noya, Barcelona

Sr Don Angel Santiago, Bodegas Rioja Santiago, S.A., Haro, Logroño

Sr Don Manuel Tapias, Bodegas Tapias, S.A., Tarragona

Sr Don Miguel Torres, Villafranca del Panadés, Barcelona

Sr Don Juan de Ugarte, Bodegas Bilbainas, S.A., Haro, Logroño

I should like to pay tribute also to my interpreter, secretary, and co-driver, Caroline Price, who, over a period of three very hard weeks in Spain, opened many doors through the fluency of her Spanish and the charm of her personality, combined with above-average knowledge of the wine we drank.

Finally, my grateful thanks are due to Yorke Crompton, for editing the book, and to Julia Trehane for the way in which she has carried out the monumental task of compiling Appendix 1.

GEORGE RAINBIRD

Foreword

I first visited Spain in 1950 with my wife, and I drove a small car down through France, entering Spain at Irún. We crossed to Burgos, and went on to Galicia and through Portugal to Seville and Jerez, and then up the Mediterranean coast, and back to England by way of Perpignan and Narbonne. We had not much money, and for economic reasons we started a habit that has persisted ever since: that of picnicking in the middle of the day. We would go to a bodega in a small town and buy a litre of the local wine, and we would shop in the market for fruit, cheese, bread, and whatever cold meat we wanted. Thereafter we chose our picnic place with a full view of some of the best scenery in the world, and enjoyed ourselves marvellously. I commend this plan.

The wine, I may add, in those days cost the equivalent of sixpence (or seven cents) a litre, and it isn't much more now. In the evenings we would drink with our dinner one of the two 'Marqueses' (Riscal or Murrieta), or perhaps a Palacio or Paternina or Santiago, usually one of the better wines of the Rioja. Thus on that trip I came to know Spanish wines at least reasonably well, and I have had a very considerable interest in them ever since.

I have been back to Spain on and off in the intervening fifteen years, and I have always drunk the common wines with appreciation and mostly with pleasure, and the better wines with considerable pleasure: hence this book. I have never found *bad* Spanish wine, which is more

than can be said for the wines of some other countries; and, in making
the fairly intense researches necessary for a book of this sort, my opinion
was confirmed that the 'faking' of wine is virtually unknown in Spain.
Spanish wines from the cheapest to the best are made simply and with
integrity, without fuss and, sometimes, in rather a slap-happy way.
This, I think, may well be one of the main reasons why the wines of
France and the wines of Spain will never really compare. Your
Spaniard is essentially a practical wine-maker, who believes in his
wine and produces it in quantity for consumption mainly by his fellow
Spaniards. He does not bring to his wine-making the philosophy and the
dedication of the Frenchman, to whom the pleasures of the table are
really a form of religion, and not a bad one at that. No, he will make
his wine honestly, and more or less with care according to the tradition
of his particular part of the country, and he will firmly believe that he
makes the best wine in all Spain. This I found to be absolutely true
throughout that pleasant land. In no place more so than in some of
the largest cooperatives, where perhaps five or six million litres of
wine are made in a year, and where last year's wine will be brought
up from every vat for one to taste and admire. Indeed, one has very
little difficulty in doing so.

One of the problems of writing this book is to give a reasonable
description of a wine so that the reader will get some idea of what to
expect. This I have found to be all but impossible, because I do not like
wine jargon, and I try to avoid it; on the other hand, Spanish wine
has suffered considerably by calling itself Sauternes or Chablis or Claret
or what have you, which it most certainly is not. And yet what do you
do? How can you convey to the reader the taste of wine unless you use
a form of comparison that he is likely to know? Therefore I have found
comparisons of this sort unavoidable, although I have used them only
sparingly. But I cannot too much emphasize that Spanish wine is
Spanish wine, and French wine is French wine, and never the twain
shall meet when they are both *in puris naturalibus*. Spanish wine will
never achieve the greatness of the great French *châteaux* or *domaines*, for
this is a matter of soil and climate more than anything else; but fine
and good wines are made everywhere in Spain, and they have their

own distinctive character, which I hope this book will encourage the reader to cultivate.

The wines of Spain are ridiculously cheap for what they are. The best wines of the Rioja are comparatively inexpensive, and the cheap wines of Valdepeñas and the Levante and Catalonia are very cheap indeed. It is not their fault that there is a swingeing tax on them of four or five times the actual cost of the wine, or that bottles cost a shilling (fourteen cents) each, and therefore they can never do the same service for England that they do for Spain, where every Spaniard can have his litre a day and afford it in whatever station of life. And does, usually, although I am told that the drinking of *mosto*, the unfermented grape-juice, is very much on the increase.

In the course of my researches, I visited all the important wine districts in Spain and at one time or another tasted all, or nearly all, the wines described in this book. When I was not able to visit a district, the Sindicato Nacional de la Vid in Madrid were kind enough to arrange for bottles to be sent to me.

I have confined to the appendices a great deal of the statistical information that is essential in a book of this sort, but might be dull reading for the layman. Nevertheless there are some figures that will no doubt interest him. The production of wine in Spain last year, for instance, was from something over 1,500,000 hectares (one hectare is about two and a half acres) of vines cultivated. This represents about 10 per cent of the total area of land cultivated in Spain, and it produces 25,000,000 hectolitres of good wine per year, as against 60,000,000 in France and 47,500,000 in Italy. The average Spaniard drinks less than the Frenchman or Italian and, I imagine, eats less too. He is a grave and sober person and sometimes eats extremely well, but always with moderation, and the same applies to his drinking habits. The cultivation of vines and the making of wines are of tremendous importance to the economy of Spain. It takes third place after cereals and olives.

Finally, let me exhort you to do your own research on the wines of Spain, preferably in their country of origin, because then you will certainly continue to buy the wines when you return home. If you do go to Spain, search out one of the little bodegas found everywhere from the smallest town upwards, where you will find anything up to twenty-four barrels of wine on tap, mostly local wine, but also wines from other parts of Spain, brandies and anises, usually with some little bits and pieces to eat on the counter; and where a glass of local wine, or of Valdepeñas, is sold for two pesetas, or about threepence in 1965 – say four cents. Sometimes you can pay as much as fourpence for a better one. Even more, perhaps; but not much more. These bodegas exist throughout Spain, and, if you are in Madrid, you should visit the narrow streets behind the Puerta del Sol, where the standard price for a glass of *blanco* or *tinto* (not a very large glass, mark you) is two pesetas. And, if you do, buy a plate of *gambas a la plancha*, which are simply luscious prawns put on to a hot plate before your eyes and served with tiny paper napkins. Tear off the head and tail of the prawn, shuck it, put it in your mouth, throw the remnants on the floor, and drink your white wine. It all sounds rather crude, but it is marvellous. Then, having visited half a dozen of these little bodegas and bars, you can go happily along to the Jockey or the Botín and have delicious sucking pig and an even more delicious bottle of fine Rioja, if you are feeling extravagant. In any case, it will not break you. But (and such is the lesson of this book) somewhere on the wine list you will find a wine – good, fine, or perhaps common – that will just suit you in whatever mood or state of affluence. You can't do that everywhere.

GEORGE RAINBIRD

Plate 2. Bridging the centuries: these vineyards near Montserrat, Barcelona, were planted when the Roman viaduct was built

Kenneth Swain

Sherry
and the Wines
of Spain

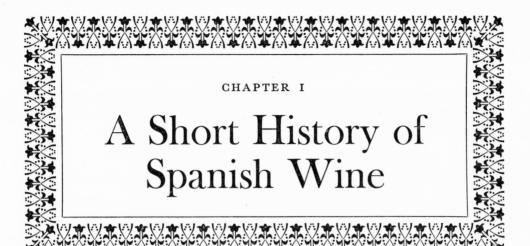

CHAPTER I

A Short History of Spanish Wine

And God said, Let the earth bring forth grass, the
herb yielding seed, and the fruit tree yielding fruit
after his kind, whose seed is in itself, upon the
earth; and it was so.

Genesis i, 11

On the third day of Creation, God put plants upon the earth in prep-
aration for the creation of mankind, and undoubtedly, in His wisdom,
He made the grape among the first of living plants. I strongly suspect
the olive was a good second, for the fruits of these two important plants
provide sustenance to mankind both physical and spiritual, to a proportion altogether greater than that of any other plant life, with the
possible exception of corn. The grape and the olive have much in
common; they thrive in hot climates and on very poor soil, and thus
provide fruit, and from the fruit drink, in places where both are otherwise hard to find. The grape, when eaten fresh from the vine, is food;
its juice, when pressed, makes a delicious drink, and when it is fermented it provides in wine a food and drink combined, which, in
moderation, can do nothing but improve the lot of man. The olive provides food and, when pressed, oil. If mankind had nothing but these, it
would at least not starve, and certainly not die of thirst.

Spain, by reason of its climate and poorish soil, has been amply provided with both vine and olive, and the history of wine-making in
Spain goes back to prehistory. There are many legends about the

discovery of wine as apart from grape-juice, but its origin, like that of the wheel, is unknown. We know that wine was used and appreciated in the most ancient days of Egypt; indeed, sealed wine jars have been found in Pharaonic tombs in the Valley of the Kings with a dusty viscous kind of mess in them, which is all that remains of the 2000 B.C. vintage of the local Cru Cléopâtre or Clos de Ptolemis. Although the early Iberian civilizations were not comparable with the Egyptian, no doubt wine was made throughout the length and breadth of Spain in the earliest days.

Edward Hyams, in his recently published book *Dionysus*, says he thinks that the first vineyards were planted in Spain before 500 B.C. I am not at all sure of his authority, and I see no reason myself why the vine should not have been cultivated long before then. Certainly the Phoenicians, who were the first settlers in Spain and who were knowledgeable about wines, could well have improved methods of viniculture. There were Greek settlements too in Spain, and no doubt there would be exchanges of ideas between all settlers and the local farmers, who have always taken some pride in making good wine. I never knew a *vigneron* yet who did not make the best wine of his country – and to blazes with all the great *châteaux* of France! William Younger, in his *Gods, Men and Wine*, gives the result of many years' patient research into the history of wine generally, including the wines of Spain, and he lists the chief ancient wine-producing areas of Spain as follows:

> Baetica
> Valdepeñas
> Barcelona and Gerona
> Valencia
> Tarragona
> The Balearic Islands
> South-west Andalusia

What we can never know is whether, for instance, the wine that was exported from Gades (modern Cádiz) and Baetica, now Andalusia, was anything like the Sherry from Jerez nearby. I would say that it very probably was, because the character of the wine is very distinctive and is partly the result of the soil, although dozens of new grapes have been introduced over the centuries. Certainly Sherry as we know it now did not really start to emerge until the end of the eighteenth century.

In Roman days (that is, from the first century B.C. onwards), wine was a major export from Spain to Rome, and it might well have been part of the tribute. In Rome today *Vinum Digatanum* may be read on amphoras of 31 B.C.; this would be the wine of Gades and would be the forerunner of the present Sherry. We also know that in the province of Baetica it was the custom to ferment and keep the wine in great Ali Baba earthenware jars called *orcae*, in which the wine of Montilla and Moriles is still kept. In the heyday of the Roman Empire, it was estimated that by the second century A.D. something like 20,000,000 amphoras of Spanish wine had been shipped into the city of Rome. The evidence of this is largely in that extraordinary artificial hill, just behind the British cemetery in Rome, called Monte Testaccio. This is the place to which I recommend that every visitor to Rome should go, even if he is there only for a couple of days. Monte Testaccio is in fact a small but substantial hill, composed simply of broken amphoras from the nearby docks on the Tiber, which was at that time navigable, and to which the ships from the Roman world brought in their tribute of oil, grain, wine, and so on. Everything in those days was carried in amphoras, with their pointed bases for standing in the earth: grain, oil, and wine. The amphoras, being of clay, were also fragile, and one imagines that the casualties on a rough voyage across the Mediterranean were enormous. Consequently, when the ship docked, the broken amphoras were carted off to what is now Monte Testaccio, and, during a thousand years or so, it became an enormous monument to the losses of ship-owners and the profits of manufacturers of amphoras. It was the custom in this period to stamp a seal on the shoulder of the amphora, usually just the initials of the owner or purveyor, and sometimes also the place of origin; and, from the proportion of these shards that can be traced to Roman Spain, we can today discover something of the extent of the wine business. Anybody can potter about Monte Testaccio if he has the energy to climb it where it stands like an enormous slag-heap – and the shards are everywhere under the sparse grass that grows on it. Some of the seals come to light with a little poking. They are very interesting and are worthy of a collection.

After the time of the Romans, the wine continued to flourish, no doubt. And then in the eighth century came the Moors, Koran in hand, preaching the pussyfoot fanaticism of Mohammed. But there is plenty of evidence that the rule of abstinence was honoured more in the breach than the observance. Quite a substantial literature, dating back to the Moorish occupation, proves that the grape was held in high esteem. Grape-juice was consumed in quantity, and fermented grape-juice, alas! also in considerable quantity. Some of the Spanish wines of this period, like the Zebbibi of Seville, had a considerable reputation, and so did the wines of Málaga, both (we note) sweet and luscious. Efforts were certainly made to extirpate the vines, but, for the purposes of this particular exercise, the Faithful became the Unfaithful, and the Faithful envied them. All sorts of dodges were employed to get round these very uncomfortable tenets of the Koran. In Córdoba, it is recorded that an arrested drunk was brought before the Chief Kadi for sentence; but he, wise man, employed a special official who, upon being asked to certify that the accused's breath smelt strongly of wine, would always say that, certainly, the man's breath smelt, but whether of grape-juice or wine it was impossible to tell. Whereupon the judge dismissed the case smartly and saved his soul from the sin of hypocrisy.

Eventually the Moors departed. People enjoyed their wine in peace; the cultivation of the grape improved, and wine was exported to France and England and, with the discovery of the New World, extensively to Mexico and Central America, where it was in demand for sacramental use in the Mass. William Younger gives a list of wines grown in and exported from medieval Spain as follows:

Alicante	From Alicante.
Caprick	From Spain or Portugal.
Espaigne	White wine.
Garnarde	Probably from Granada, in the fourteenth century.
Lepe	Probably from ancient Illipula (modern Niebla), between Seville and Huelva; it could also be a general term for wine coming from, or through, Seville.
Málaga	Málaga wine.
Ordiales	From Castro Urdiales, Province of Santander.
Osey	From Spain and Portugal.
Ryvere	From the River Ebro – possibly modern Rioja; from Logroño and

nearby parts, but more probably Zaragoza and Tarragona. It was also called a wine 'of the river'.

Tente	From Spain certainly.
Torrentyne	From the River Ebro (*see* Ryvere above).
Xérès	From Jerez de la Frontera.

Of these wines, Málaga is probably the best-known today. Tente has long gone out, although it survived into the nineteenth century. The Lepe was much loved of Chaucer, who mentions it on several occasions, but especially in:

> Now kepe yow fro the whyte and fro the rede,
> And namely fro the whyte wine of Lepe,
> That is to selle in Fish-strete or in Chepe.
> This wyn of Spayne crepeth subtilly
> In othere wynes, growing faste by,
> Of which ther ryseth swich fumositee,
> That whan a man hath dronken draughtes three,
> And weneth that he be at hoom in Chepe,
> He is in Spayne, right at the toune of Lepe,
> Nat at the Rochel, ne at Burdeux toun.

Lepe indeed may well have some affinity with the Sherry of today. From that time onwards, the wine of Spain became fairly well noted and quoted throughout the literature of Spain. It is recorded that in 1237 Ordiales was bought for Henry III of England, while in 1358 good Spanish wine cost sixpence (seven cents) a gallon in England; but this might well have been expensive. The history of Sack, which was the wine of Shakespeare's day, I shall deal with in the next chapter. I shall give a certain amount of historical information there and in later chapters, as being more suitable places for it than this general introduction.

Comparatively modern authors have dealt with Spanish wine, continuing in the tradition of Cervantes. To conclude this brief introduction, I must add that I could not but be delighted to find that the pigskins of wine so horribly slashed and gored by Don Quixote are still largely in use in La Mancha. Traditions and customs die hard in conservative Spain. May this one, with its roots deep in history, never die.

CHAPTER 2

Sherry

Sherris, Scheris, Xérès, or Jerez – whatever you may call it, it ends up as Sherry. And this incomparable wine is probably the greatest jewel in the crown of Spanish wines. As its name denotes, it comes from that part of Western Andalusia of which Jerez de la Frontera is the principal town, but the *denominación de origen* areas also include Sanlúcar de Barrameda, famous for its *manzanillas*, and Puerto de Santa María, and stretches as far as Chiclana in the south and up to the Guadalquivir river in the north. Not so long ago, the district was very much larger, and places like Niebla and Manzanilla (from which no *manzanilla* comes now) could and did export their wine as Sherry; but this has all been stopped, with some considerable hardship, I am told, to the inhabitants.

Sherry wines are made in the surrounding country and taken to the great bodegas in Jerez, Puerto de Santa María, and Sanlúcar de Barrameda for blending into that glorious wine we all know as Sherry. For Sherry is not a complete wine; it is in fact a blend of wines that have some affinity, and it is normally a fortified wine, by which is meant that grape-brandy is added at some stage in the fermenting process. Consequently we must examine at considerable length the whole process of making Sherry wine, so that we may understand its peculiar and especially good qualities, which have made it renowned throughout the world, and which distinguish Jerez from parts of Spain that produce by the same process a wine that is not the true Sherry wine.

28

Plate 3. A Macharnudo vineyard, near Jerez
Kenneth Swain

The wines of Jerez appear in the most ancient chronicles of the times of the Phoenicians and the Romans. So do they also in most of the other parts of Spain, especially on the Mediterranean coast. It was not until 1635 or thereabouts that the wine became known as Sherry; before that it appeared chiefly in the Elizabethan form of Sack or Sherris Sack. Shakespeare is simply full of it, and every schoolboy knows that it was Falstaff's favourite tipple by a long way. Throughout *Henry IV*, Parts 1 and 2, Falstaff needs no encouragement to launch forth into praise of Sack, of which he drinks aplenty and all the time. 'O monstrous! but one half-pennyworth of bread to this intolerable deal of sack!' exclaims Prince Hal, examining Falstaff's enormous bill for a party at the Boar's Head Tavern with a few gallons of Sack and a very small amount of bread.

> We care not for money, riches or wealth,
> Old sack is our money, old sack is our wealth,

wrote Thomas Randolph in praise of old Sack.

Sack in those days was drunk by the pint and normally in tankards drawn straight from the barrel, but it need not necessarily have come from Jerez or even Spain, for a great deal of a similar type of wine was imported from the Canaries; there seems, however, to be little doubt that the very great popularity of Sack led eventually – in Victorian days, when many of them were founded – to the prosperity of the great Anglo-Spanish houses. In one of these John Ruskin's father was a partner. Its success enabled him to provide his son with a more than liberal education, and thus made possible his writings, which in their turn made a tremendous impression for good on Victorian life and letters.

An anonymous poet of the seventeenth century wrote:

> Then let us drink old sacke, boyes,
> Which makes us fond and merry,
> The life of mirth and joy on earth,
> Is a cuppe of good old sherry.

Just exactly what the Sack of those great and hard-drinking days was like we shall never know, because although Sherries (I suppose by reason of their being fortified) do last to a very great age, they won't last for centuries. There are, however, soleras in Jerez that are authenticated back well into the middle of the eighteenth century. Whether or not the famous Williams & Humbert 'Dry Sack' has any affinity with Falstaff's Sack is purely a matter of conjecture. I imagine, for instance, that the Sherry of today might well be stronger than it was then, and yet undoubtedly any wine made by the solera system and using the grapes and the methods of Jerez will be of very high alcoholic content.

The vineyards that supply the wines made into Sherry lie adjacent rather than close to the three principal towns, and, as has been pointed out by Rupert Croft-Cooke in his excellent book on Sherry, the vineyards are not apparent from the road or the railway. There are two major areas between Jerez de la Frontera and the Guadalquivir river. One comprises the districts of Carrascal and, more importantly, Macharnudo; and the other, further west, Miraflores and Balbaina. South of Jerez de la Frontera, Puerto de Santa María, and the River Guadalete are those vineyards near Puerto Real, San Fernando, and Chiclana; and other patches lie further inland.

There are three kinds of soil, some of them almost together in quite a small area, and the chief of these soils is called *albariza*, a fine chalky soil with which one soon becomes smothered when walking round the vineyards in Macharnudo. It is undoubtedly this remarkable soil that makes this remarkable wine, just as the rather heavier chalky soil of Champagne makes Champagne, and the pebbly sand of the Médoc makes the greatest claret in the world. The *albarizas* are the best soils; though they produce the fewest grapes per vine, they are essential for the making of *finos*, which are the basis of most Jerez wines and the most important. After the vines grown on the *albarizas* are those grown on the *barros*, which are much less chalky soils but are more prolific. After the *barros* come the *arenas* – sandy types of soil, producing a great many more grapes to the vine than either the *barros* or the *albarizas*; but all play their part, and we must appreciate their importance against the background of the solera system by which they are blended.

After the soil, we have the sun. In this respect, the region round Jerez de la Frontera is probably one of the most favoured in Spain. The rainfall is light, and only in an exceptional year will there be more than eighty to a hundred days in which rain will fall. I remember when I was there some years ago, in mid-October, the few showers that descended were the first since the previous April; the grapes had been gathered, and this was considered absolutely right for the making of good wine. The rain will, however, be quite heavy for nearly a month or two; then the sun will begin to shine uninterruptedly again in the very early spring. This climatic condition has been taken care of in the system of vine-planting, whereby a plot a metre or so square is excavated to a very great depth indeed, and the chalky soil is pulverized, mixed with humus, and heaped round the stump of the vine to form a kind of porous bed, into which the winter rains seep and maintain some degree of moisture during the long summer when the vines will flower and the grapes form and eventually ripen. This method is adopted throughout Spain; but, so far as I know, the depth of the excavation is usually not more than a metre, whereas in the Jerez district some two and a half to three metres may be dug before planting the vine. So much for soil and sun.

Next we have the grapes. According to Rupert Croft-Cooke, there are records that numerous types of grapes, including some black ones, were used until a hundred years or more ago; but this has now changed, and the two principal grapes used in Jerez, besides the common Cana-cazo and Mollar varieties, are the Palomino, which is used for the *finos* and the *amontillados*, and the Pedro Ximénez or P.X. grape used largely for the *olorosos* and the dessert wine of the same name. The Palomino is essentially a grape of the Sherry district and is eminently suitable to *albariza* soil, which makes *finos*, while the Pedro Ximénez grapes are grown in some quantity more or less all over Spain, especially where sweet wines are made.

Normally in the Jerez district the vintage will begin around the 9th of September and go on until the end of the month or possibly early October, both according to the season and to the grapes, because some grapes are gathered much earlier than others. The grapes are cut, not with the scissors or little shears used elsewhere, but with sharp knives. I don't know why this should be, and I doubt very much whether the vintagers of Jerez do either, but it is the traditional instrument for the job, and so it goes on from year to year.

The bodegas in which the wines are made will invariably be found near the middle of the vineyard, and they are usually composed of a long whitewashed tiled building, with a covered courtyard in which stands the platform where the treading of the grapes is done, while outside there is a pretty big expanse, a kind of terrace or apron, upon which the picker will unload his grapes on to large, circular hempen mats, where they are left to dry for a day or so in the strong Andalusian sunlight. At this stage the grapes are 'plastered' by a small quantity of gypsum that is sprinkled on them, although I believe this part of the operation is not always carried out. Certainly the enemies of Sherries in the past have made great play with the 'plastering' of Sherry wine, but the gypsum additive is so small as to have no particular significance so far as the essential quality of the wine is concerned. At night the grapes are covered with another mat to stop the dew from damping them, and to ensure that they are quite dry when they go into the *lagar* or wine-press.

The *lagares* are wooden troughs twelve feet square with sides, as far as I can remember, about two feet high, and with a slightly sloping floor and holes through which the pressed *mosto* or must pours after the treading. The men who tread the grapes are called *pisadores*, and they are splendidly tough specimens clad in bathing trunks and singlets, wearing otherwise only their berets and iron-shod shoes called *zapatos*. They have wooden shovels, and they marshal the grapes, brought in on mats, into great heaps in the *lagar*. When they have arranged them to their satisfaction, they start their one-two rhythmic tread, systematically working through the grapes and treading them with their *zapatos*. It takes a little time for the juice to start running, but gradually the stream increases as the treading becomes more intense. This operation is necessarily lengthy, but it is none the less thorough and goes on for hours at a time. The iron studs in the *zapatos* are arranged with enough space between them to ensure that, when the treading takes place, the pips and stalks and skins will not be bruised, to affect the must with an addition of tannin contained in those parts of the grape. Sometimes the treading of the grapes is accompanied – I suppose to alleviate boredom – by a traditional treading-song, which is nothing if not Andalusian, punctuated by the double mark-time of the treaders. They do not sing this all the while, but, since they may be treading grapes for four or more hours at a time with intervals for changing the grapes, they certainly need the Spanish equivalent of the Song of the Volga Boatmen.

After the *pisadores* have extracted all the juice they possibly can from the grapes, the resulting mess of pips, skins, and the rest is shovelled first of all into hand-presses for a second pressing, which produces a certain amount, and then into mechanical presses for yet a third pressing, which produces a little more; this, however, is not added to the original must, but kept either for distillation or for making an inferior quality of wine. The grape-juice from the first and second pressings is put straight into butts, and is left in the sun to start its fermentation before being removed to the bodegas, possibly some miles away, in Jerez, Puerto de Santa María, or Sanlúcar de Barrameda. The scene along the roads at vintage time is remarkable, with the heavy tumbrils, drawn by teams of long-horned oxen, hauling the great butts of wine, which have started the fermentation that will one day make them into some of the greatest wine in the world.

At this stage, something must be said about the Sherry butt and its importance to the wine contained in it. Air and oxygenization are more essential in Sherry than in almost any other wine, mainly for the development of the yeast and organisms contained in the 'flower' and so on. Consequently the butt in which the wine is matured needs to have a certain porous quality, even though, obviously, the vessel must be watertight. Therefore all the bodegas have a very important cooperage department, making as many of their own butts and casks as they can, though they usually have to buy some. This is becoming increasingly difficult through the shortage of the right kind of oak, but I expect the Sherry trade will cope with it, although costs are rising all the time. So, for that matter, is the price of Sherry. I suppose I could take two or three pages to describe the technical intricacies of making a good Sherry butt; suffice it to say that they are necessarily of the best possible construction, and have built into them those qualities that have been designed over a few hundred years as being ideal first of all for the maturing and then the transportation of the wine.

In some parts of Spain, the new butt is matured by filling it with sea-water for three weeks or so; but I never heard that this was done in Jerez, where the normal practice is to fill it with *mosto* until it is thoroughly soaked.

The great bodegas of Jerez, most of which were built or expanded in the prosperity of the nineteenth century, and which I shall discuss in detail later, are really tremendous: great cathedral-like naves with butts five or six deep, each containing more than a hundred gallons, in rows two or three hundred yards long. These, however, are the soleras, and the new wine that has just come from the *lagares* is left until it has finished its first tumultuous fermentation and gone through most of its second; that is to say, in two or three months.

During this time is formed that unique but essential element of the true Sherry *fino*, the 'flower'. The 'flower' forms at the end of the secondary fermentation. It is a kind of scum composed of yeasts and ferments on the top of the wine, and it stays there and increases during its whole period in butt before the final blending; you see it in the form of tiny specks of matter in the maturing wine. It is difficult to describe, but it is everywhere present even when the wine is fortified, always provided too much alcohol is not added, because the alcohol kills the 'flower', and people generally consider that it is the 'flower' that gives the true *fino* its essential character and quality.

It is at this stage – that is to say, when the first and secondary fermentations have finished and the wine has become clear – that the head of the bodega will classify it according to its quality, and will mark the butt by a series of strokes and cross-strokes; in accordance with the marking, it will be allocated to the solera most suited to the wine. The classification will be explained later, when *finos* are discussed.

The wine has now been allocated and classified according to the taster's judgement, and it will be put into new butts that have been fumigated with sulphur, and that will have in them the degree of alcohol considered necessary to bring the wine up to the required standard of vinosity and to stop further fermentation. It should be noted that this wine-alcohol, which I suppose could be termed brandy, is used only sparingly in the *fino* wines. This is called fortification. At least two of the Jerez bodegas do not fortify their wines at all for the domestic market, and do it for the English market only to enable the wines to travel. The resulting *finos* are extremely delicate and fine, and, while it might be a degree or so below standard in alcoholic strength, it is certainly a delicious wine. The odd thing about it is that I find this practice of making unfortified Sherry universally denied throughout Spain, yet I know it to exist, and I personally like the natural wine very much indeed.

The grapes have been pressed; the wine has been made and has been allocated to a solera, and will take its place as a member of the choir in one of the great cathedrals of Jerez. For that really is what a solera is.

The time has come to discuss in detail the solera system upon which these great wines are made, and this is simply a matter of superb blending of young and old wines. No matter which types of wine are bought from Jerez de la Frontera, Puerto de Santa María, or Sanlúcar de Barrameda, they one and all have been made by the solera system, and it is these great soleras that constitute the wealth of the whole district. It would be almost impossible now for a new bodega to start making Sherry unless its owners had been able to buy an existing solera. I must explain this mystery.

Sherry is essentially a blended wine. The blending is both vertical and horizontal, by which I mean that old wine is blended with new wine, and new wines are blended with other new wines of a similar but not always of an identical character. The solera starts with a few butts, sometimes of a given year, and, as years go on, more butts are added to the solera; so, to produce a standard-quality wine (such as – shall we say? – the 'Tío Pepe' of González Byass or the 'Macharnudo Fino' of La Riva, the first selling in enormous and the second in substantial quantities), the solera would necessarily be of many, many hundred butts. A certain quantity of wine, possibly a third or a half, is taken from the oldest butts, and these are filled with wine from the next oldest, and so on, right down the enormous row. Thus the oldest and best elements in the wine are always present in proportion to the quality of the wine required.

The matching of wine before entry into a solera is yet another thing again; and here the Sherry-taster reigns supreme with his cane, called a *venencia*, which is a metre-long piece of whalebone with a silver cup at one end and a hook at the other to save it from falling into the butt. The taster will thrust the *venencia* into the bung-hole at the top of the barrel, through the 'flower' that has already formed, then bring a sample up in the tiny cup from the middle of the butt, and pour it into his *copita* or tasting-glass at arm's length without spilling a single drop. Obviously, in the case of a very popular Sherry, selling in enormous quantities, the wine will not be terribly old, neither is it desirable that it should be so, though it would normally not be less than about three years old. On the other hand, most of the older bodegas have what corresponds to the 'paradise' of the brandy-shippers of Cognac, and also have a little private solera of only two or three butts, which are broached maybe once a year, and which are known to have been started anything up to a couple of hundred years ago. These wines, I need hardly say, are not sold, but are kept for state occasions and opened only rarely, tapped lightly, and refreshed from wine nearly as old.

The truly remarkable wine that I had the pleasure and privilege of tasting from the La Riva private cellar goes back to 1770. It is very dark and absolutely dry, and there is a crust so fine as to be no more than a misting in the bottle, which, even taking the greatest possible care, I find extremely hard to decant without disturbing, and I have to use a filter paper on the very rare occasions when I open one of my few remaining half-bottles.

Again, as with Cognac, the very old soleras are normally used only for blending and to give tremendous character to younger wines. The oldest soleras are *amontillados*, *olorosos*, or Pedro Ximénez. *Finos* cease to be *finos* after a few generations and become with age true *amontillados*, which can be very dry and a little nutty and are delicious. The *olorosos*, which are made as a rule from the Pedro Ximénez grapes, are sweet (but this I will discuss later on), while a true solera of 'Uncle Peter', or Pedro Ximénez, has the consistency of lubricating oil and a cloying sweetness that I find quite impossible, although there are some who like it.

Thus the wine of Jerez de la Frontera and district has been famous

Plate 4. The making of Sherry: classifying the wine

Kenneth Swain

for centuries, but when exactly the present system of wine-making known as the solera system was introduced we do not know for certain; it is, however, generally agreed as having been in the eighteenth century. At one time, no doubt, the wine was just a natural wine of the country (the local *vino de mesa*, as it were), and this might well have been in Shakespeare's day. Possibly the grapes were left to become overripe and fermented, and were then pressed; the wine would be clarified and shipped. Somewhere along the line the solera system was perfected, probably in the last half of the eighteenth century, but exactly when is not known by any of the Sherry experts with whom I have discussed the problem.

So we have the vast bodegas and the enormous soleras of these three towns. When the time has come, the Sherry is racked from the solera, usually from the lower tier of the *fino* solera, and put into a standard butt of 108 gallons (the solera butt is somewhat larger) and shipped off to England or wherever its final destination may be, to delight connoisseurs all over the world. For domestic use and South American countries, the Sherry is usually sold in bottles. And very bright some of them are, completely encased in gold or silver foil, or with lovely gold silk netting and large red tassels. The wine therein is usually rather on the sweet side for our taste.

TYPES OF SHERRY WINE

There are three basic types of Sherry, with various sub-divisions up and down throughout. These types are essentially the *fino*, the *oloroso*, and a third type that I classify as a Pedro Ximénez, which in a way is a form of *oloroso*, but is, I feel, so individual as to make a class by itself. An easy distinction is that the *fino*, with its sub-classification of *amontillado* and *manzanilla*, is essentially dry and usually pale; the *olorosos* are dark and rather sweet, and of course Pedro Ximénez is very sweet indeed. There are great wines in each of these classes, and most of the big shippers make Sherry in them all.

The true *fino* is very, very pale, with a hint of gold. Before it is

c

finally bottled, the specks of the *flor* or 'flower' are present in it. It is always dry, and for the domestic market it is sometimes unfortified. It may be drunk, as it is in its best qualities, as an aperitif before lunch or dinner; in its more common varieties it is served purely as a drinking wine, especially in the bars. If you order *vino tinto* in a bar anywhere in Spain, you get just that, the *corriente* or common red wine of the district, or possibly you get Valdepeñas. If, however, you order *vino blanco*, you will in all probability get a cheap *fino* Sherry, and there won't be any difference in the cost. These *corrientes finos* are excellent wines, with very little acidity and no roughness, and I have drunk them with a great deal of pleasure, whereas I could not possibly drink the better Sherries as I did the *corriente* Sherry in Spain. If you want a simple white wine, you must always be very careful to ask for a *vino blanco de mesa*. *Finos* are usually rated at between 15° and 16° of alcohol, and they have a further technical sub-division, which may be called 'palmas', and are simply *finos* from Jerez or Puerto de Santa María of good quality. With the exception of the La Riva 'Tres Palmas', I do not know of any other brand that uses the technical division as a brand name: this is mostly used within the bodega to denote the quality before marketing under the bodega's own special *marque*, and it can be one *palma*, two *palmas*, three *palmas*, or four *palmas*. If you see Sherry marked *cuatro palmas*, you should buy it because it is about the best there is.

Manzanilla wine comes from Sanlúcar de Barrameda at the mouth of the Guadalquivir river, a small port where some of the ships stand in before going up to Seville; alternatively, if they are too large, they may take off their cargoes from Andalusia. There is also a fishing village attached, on rather good sands, and I remember eating at a restaurant actually on those sands a most delightful fish meal, in which course after course of splendid fish was served Chinese fashion, to the complement of jugs of new, young *manzanilla* of excellent genus, browny-gold and with the faintly nutty taste that makes it an altogether excellent and exceptional *fino*. Just exactly why *manzanilla* should have this distinctive quality, I have never quite discovered, because the grapes are the same and the soil is much the same. I suppose it must be bred into it in the local formula for vinification. Long may it reign!

The oldest *finos* become *amontillados*, but *amontillados* need not be old. To make up the *amontillado* soleras, the grapes for this type of wine are gathered a few days earlier, and they remain therefore somewhat dry. *Fino*, being left in butt for a long time, automatically becomes *amontillado* and develops its own very special and distinctive flavour, while retaining its extreme dry qualities; it is from *finos* that have grown old naturally in butts that the *amontillado* soleras have been made up over a few generations. Some *amontillados* grow to a very great age, and I should think they will keep for ever. In Córdoba, which is where the bodegas of Montilla and Moriles are situated, they will tell you that *amontillado* really comes from their district; hence the name Montilla forms part of the word *amontillado*. This is hotly, if not bitterly, contested in Jerez, where people deny that the Córdobans could possibly make such good wine as *amontillado*. My advice is that the reader should go to a little trouble and try the Córdoba variety as well as the Jerez; he might get a pleasant surprise. But I am all for *amontillado* as a clean, dry, altogether satisfactory wine, whether it comes from Jerez or Montilla.

Olorosos are wines that are made mainly from the Palomino grapes, but with a proportion of Pedro Ximénez grapes; fermentation is stopped, while the wines are still quite sweet, by the addition of alcohol. There is an internal qualitative classification of these wines, as there is in the case of *finos*, but, instead of specifying different qualities of *palmas*, the makers use the word *cortado*, and the wine is classified for bodega purposes as anything between one and four *cortados*. Again, the only firm I know that markets an *oloroso* under the *cortado* label is La Riva; the wine is called 'Tres Cortados', which is the equivalent in *oloroso* to the 'Tres Palmas' in *fino*, but it is not so sweet as some *olorosos* and is excellent with game soup. *Olorosos* are not necessarily all sweet wines, although most of them are, mainly because the public expect them to be. A great many of the old East India Sherries were *olorosos*, and the reason for their name is that people thought the sea voyage of some months helped to age the Sherry and give it a special quality; consequently the great butts of *oloroso* were sometimes sent to the East Indies and back via London, and the wines received a better price. It was possibly a better wine.

I had a very small bin of such wine some years ago, and I used to bring it out at eleven o'clock on Christmas morning, which seemed to be the right occasion, together with a mince-pie. It was an extremely rich but by no means sickly Sherry, which was looked forward to by the whole family until, alas! the last bottle was consumed about two Christmases ago. I am looking for some more to take its place now, but the fashion of sending Sherry to the East Indies has long gone out, and I haven't heard of it for many years. If you should come across it, you can be sure you will have a very old and probably very good Sherry. Pray let me into the secret, as I should like to buy some more.

The last class, and it could possibly be a sub-division of the *olorosos*, is the Sherry made entirely from the Pedro Ximénez grape, and with its fermentation stopped long before the sugar has been broken down into alcohol, thus retaining its almost sickly sweetness. I am no lover of Pedro Ximénez (or P.X., as it is called), because I don't like wines that cloy, and P.X. certainly does. There is no question about its superb quality, but I have never yet found a peach sweet enough to eat with it, and it will kill the taste of even its own grape.

The famous Bristol *marques* of Sherry – that is, the 'Milk', which may come from Harveys, Averys, or any Bristol shipper, and the 'Cream', which I believe can only be sold under that name by Harveys – are all of the rich *oloroso* dessert type of wine. As might be expected, they constitute the best of these wines. Vast quantities are shipped all over the world from Puerto de Santa María, which is the port of Jerez, and they have done more for Sherry and for Bristol than almost any other kind of wine.

Any other forms of Sherry can be considered as *marques* of the particular bodega rather than the type of wine. 'Tío Pepe', for instance, is simply a *fino* with its own particular character; 'Dry Sack', which is not terribly dry, is an *amontillado*, and 'Walnut Brown' is an *oloroso*. Each of these famous names has been blended by the shipper from his own soleras to suit his market and in the best ways he knows how.

Hence the great names and the great Sherries have spread, from Jerez to Puerto de Santa María and Sanlúcar de Barrameda, through the length and breadth of the civilized world.

The alcoholic content of Sherry varies a great deal, but as a general guide we can take something like the following:

Finos	From 15° to 16°.
Amontillados	From 16° to 18°, rising at times, according to age and vinification, to 20°, and in very exceptional cases even 24°.
Olorosos	Starting at about 18° to 20° and rising sometimes to 24°.
Pedro Ximénez	Rarely less than between 20° and 24°, and, in the case of a very old solera, rising perhaps even higher.

THE GREAT SHERRY BODEGAS

I do not know how many bodegas there are in Jerez – indeed, large and small, there must be hundreds; but the greatest of them, and those that are responsible for nearly all the exports, particularly to England, while having their roots in Spain, have considerable British interests, both financial and commercial. The more insular Spaniard has not allowed the infusion of British blood in the same way as Port shippers have done in Oporto; at least, not nearly to the same extent. It is true the great firm of Williams & Humbert is British in origin, but this is an exception rather than the rule; and, while (as in the case of Domecq, through the redoubtable Ruskin senior) a few firms have British connections, the firms are essentially Spanish, keeping their commercial contacts with collaborators in London through the agency system, which, in the case of Sherry, has always worked extremely well and amicably.

Jerez de la Frontera is a large town of, I suppose, about 100,000 inhabitants; I also suppose it could be one of the most prosperous towns in Spain outside Madrid. Its well-ordered streets, its squares and gardens, its ancient honey-coloured churches and buildings, together with the *palacios* of what Mr Croft-Cooke calls the Sherry barons, make it an altogether pleasant place. The principal hotel, under the sign of Los Cisnes, is extremely comfortable and, naturally enough, it displays some hundreds of different Sherries collected from every bodega in town, and some outside it. There is also a formidable list of Spanish wines, especially from the Rioja.

The heat in Andalusia is something quite remarkable, and the town shuts down between midday and four o'clock in the afternoon, after which hour things start coming to life again. Nothing moves at any speed, least of all the rumbling tumbrils of Sherry, still often hauled by long-horned oxen, but inside the white walls of these great bodegas, with their row upon mighty row of maturing Sherry, little seems to happen at any time. Inside a bodega, indeed, there is usually a court-yard, perhaps there are two or more courtyards, often with orange trees, and many are filled with bougainvillea and other lovely exotic flowers; at least one shipper is reputed to grow jasmine in his bodega, hoping that something of its delicate scent will work itself into the wine. I should like to think this was possible.

The larger bodegas, especially the exporting ones, have two things in common: a tremendous sense of hospitality, and a carefully contrived bar at which the welcome visitor will be asked to 'look' at the wine of the bodega after being shown over the establishment. Very little formality is needed for a visit of this sort, although a letter of introduc-tion from a local wine merchant is by no means a bad thing to have. Moreover, in the case of the great bodegas, language does not present any particular problem. This is unusual, because the essential language in Spain is Spanish, and, elsewhere in the bodegas of Spain, even in the very large ones, to find anybody speaking English is the exception rather than the rule.

The particular *marques* of the great bodegas are a matter entirely for the bodegas themselves and originate in their own soleras. Many of these brands started long, long ago; each indicates a particular character of Sherry, one that the proprietor at the time thought best suited to his trade and to public demand. All the wine produced must come under the three general classifications already discussed, but some of the deviations are extremely interesting, especially those blended for the South American market. A list of Sherry-exporters and their principal brands will be found in Appendix 3.

Those best known in England must be mentioned: firms like the giant González Byass y Cía, whose world-famous 'Tío Pepe' (Tío Pepe is re-puted to have been the founder of the firm) is known wherever Sherry is drunk. Sandeman Brothers are as well known for their Sherries as for their Ports; and Williams & Humbert, whose name speaks of the British foundation of an Anglo-Spanish firm, have their 'Dry Sack' and 'Walnut Brown' Sherries, which are also as famous as they are excellent. Another Jerez giant, Pedro Domecq, comes in here with 'La Ina' *fino* and, of course, a list of Spanish brandies, of which more in the appropriate chapter. Osborne of Puerto de Santa María was founded in 1772, and markets the famous 'El Cid' Sherry and many others. The house of Terry, also in Puerto de Santa María, market the Sherry of that name and also the formidable Puerto de Santa María brandy. In Puerto de Santa María, the Duff Gordon Company was really founded by Sir James Duff, the British Consul in Cádiz at the end of the eighteenth century, although his family no longer control the Spanish side of the business. The firm of M. Ant. de la Riva has the longest history in Jerez; although it may have existed earlier, since 1776 it has been passed down from father to son, and the family is happy in the ownership of some of the oldest soleras in the town. It is not a big concern as compared with the Jerez giants, but it certainly has excellent wine; its *fino* 'Tres Palmas' is a perfect example of this type of wine. They also market an excellent *manzanilla* called 'M.Z.A. La Riva', and some superb *olorosos*, amongst them 'Guadalupe Amontillado' (from the vineyards of that district), which is an excellent wine of its type when drunk with a really strong soup.

In Sanlúcar de Barrameda, the home of *manzanilla*, the firm of Antonio Barbadillo, S.A., is among the best, but González Byass have also a very large bodega, in which they have soleras of this special and altogether charming wine. Most of the Jerez bodegas have somewhat smaller installations here, but there are also many local firms.

SHERRY IN ENGLAND

I suggest that, if you asked which was the best-known Sherry throughout the world, the answer would be 'Bristol Cream', which is the *marque* so well established by Harvey's. This company was built up in Bristol at the end of the eighteenth century by a long line of sea-captains and ship-owners, most of whom no doubt brought back as cargo the wines of Spain, and especially Sherry. Now Harvey's dominate the trade with this *oloroso* dessert wine, which they have made very much their own; but the Bristol Milk, which is more of a generic term for certain *oloroso* wines, can be bought elsewhere. Avery's of Bristol, for example, also have an excellent Bristol Milk; so do one or two other Bristol firms. Unlike the other firms, however, Harvey's maintain their own bodegas both in Jerez and Montilla.

Something should certainly be said here about the Sherry imported directly from Jerez by reputable wine-merchants throughout the length and breadth of the land, and marketed under their own particular trade-names. It would be impossible to supply a complete list, because, in every town where there are cultured and intelligent people, you will nearly always find a cultured and intelligent wine-merchant who has, over the years, had his own particular mark of Sherry blended for him in Jerez, and has imported it in bulk and bottled it himself, selling it under his own name. It is easy to come by one or two examples of this, such as the 'Elizabeta' of Avery's of Bristol, which is an extremely good *fino* from Jerez, and the equal of many of the *grandes marques* marketed under the Spanish label; Findlater, Mackie, Todd are famous for their 'Dry Fly', and Grants of St James's also have a wide range. I cannot therefore do more than recommend that you buy from your local wine-merchant a bottle of his own brand, and match it with the larger ones. Your personal taste will decide the issue.

There are hundreds of good Sherries coming from Jerez, and the best recommendation I can possibly make is that people should ask for them through their local wine-merchants and find out for themselves. I append a list of the important wine-shippers, together with their famous *marques*, and the types of wine those *marques* represent. Choose, if you like, a different one every time. They will all be good.

CHAPTER 3

The Wines of
Montilla and Moriles

The wines of Montilla and Moriles – they are practically the same thing – deserve to be a great deal better known outside Spain, and especially in England, than they are, although it is possible that they have often been drunk by people who have never heard the name or known whence they came. Roses by any other name would smell as sweet.

I have always known these wines as the Sherries of Córdoba, for Córdoba is the commercial centre of the area where some of the bodegas are situated, and it is the distributing centre for the whole district. The wines not only have an affinity with the true Sherry of Jerez, but are almost identical with it. Montilla can be, and is, blended to match all the standard grades of Sherry, and, while there is a basic difference in the method of making, as we shall see, the result is so similar as to be practically indistinguishable to the lay palate. There is one big difference in that all the wines of Montilla and Moriles have no addition whatever of alcohol, even for export, in contradistinction to Jerez wines, which although sometimes entirely pure for the domestic market, are otherwise nearly always fortified by the addition of grape alcohol to bring them up to the required standard of alcoholic content and to stabilize their keeping and travelling qualities. True Montilla seems to need no help in this respect, and I have in my own cellar the remnants of a small bin that I bought in the Ashburnham House sale some years ago, after it had lain in that cellar since 1875.

49

All of it, so far, has been perfectly sound, very slightly *maderisé*, bone-dry, and quite delicious.

Córdoba has, as is well known, a long history under Phoenician, Roman, Moorish, and Spanish rulers. Its wine was well known in Rome, where it was served to the Caesars, and Munda – the name of the present Montilla – was a thriving Roman town; there is even evidence that an amphora, bearing the seal of Munda, and undoubtedly containing Montilla of that day, has been excavated recently in Italy. This need not be surprising, as none of the wines of Italy approximate in any way to the special qualities of the Andalusian wine, and the Caesars, who were always on the look-out for special kinds of food and drink to break the monotony of their table, would certainly go to the trouble of shipping in a few amphoras to impress their friends. Whether or not the viniculture suffered under the Moors is problematical, for, while the Koran lays down that there was a devil in every berry of the grape, evidence exists that these particular devils were not despised, especially in Córdoba, for many Arab writers have extolled the virtue of wine in general and of Montilla in particular.

The area in which Montilla wine is made reaches far north of Córdoba, but in practice these northern vineyards, fifty miles from Córdoba itself, do not produce the characteristic wines of the region. The true Montilla and Moriles wines come from grapes grown in and around the villages of Montilla, Aguilar, Cabra, Puente Genil, and Lucena. Moriles itself is a tiny village, but it gives its name to an administrative region. Montilla, on the other hand, is a thriving town of about 25,000 people, in which can be found upwards of a hundred bodegas, although only about fifteen are of a substantial size. Whether they be large or small, however, the wine is made to a system corresponding almost exactly with the making of the wine and the blending processes of the Jerez system. Thus, as in Jerez, the great value of the wine derives from its having been produced by established and often very ancient soleras, which are quite irreplaceable and without which fine wines cannot be made. This has already been explained in the chapter on Jerez.

Unlike Jerez, however, this wine is one in which virtually only a single type of grape is used, the Pedro Ximénez, which accounts for more than 90 per cent of the wine; a very small amount of Lairén and Moscatel grapes is also used. In Jerez, the Pedro Ximénez grape is associated nearly always with the richer and sweeter *oloroso* soleras and with the Pedro Ximénez wine. Rarely, if ever is it used for the *finos* and *amontillados*, but in Montilla the grape is used universally, and the finest wines are completely dry, because fermentation is allowed to go its full course and the grapes are not sun-dried after picking; the sugar in the grape is transmuted into alcohol and does not retain its sweetness.

The best wines of Montilla and Moriles come from the Sierra de Montilla, and the Moriles Alto. The grapes are grown on arid, chalky, intensely white soil, which, while having a small yield, certainly produces the finest wines. Some care and skill are applied in the blending of the two wines in the great bodegas, and it is said that the wines of Moriles can be likened to a strong, handsome man and the wines from the Sierra de Montilla to a very beautiful girl; the resulting combination is all that might be expected of such a union. In point of fact, the Moriles wines are fractionally sharper (to say that they are bitter would be to put it too strongly), but both wines have very considerable character. There is a tiny glint of green in the gold of the wine; it is not always present in Sherry, and I found it very attractive. Indeed, I have always found Montilla a very attractive wine.

The vines are planted, more or less as in Jerez, by digging out a cubic metre of soil, pulverizing it, and mixing it well with humus before replacing it; the vine is then planted in the centre, thus making a kind of pocket, which will assimilate the winter rains and retain a degree of moisture during the long, hard, and intensely hot summer, for it is said that Córdoba is the hottest corner of Spain. The vines are pruned down to four or six shoots, and the vintage is somewhat earlier than in most parts of Spain. I saw the last grapes from the 1965 harvest unloaded at the press-house on the 22nd of September, at which time the vintage had not begun in some bodegas in Valdepeñas, 150 miles to the north, and was still a month away in other parts of Spain.

The Bodegas Alvear in Montilla have two fine modern bodegas, and in one everything was over; the place had been swept clean and all the presses and the crushing machinery had been washed up for another year. In the other, some seven or eight kilometres into Moriles Alto, the last load was being delivered with the customary cheerful bustle. The smell of fermenting grapes hung heavily on both bodegas.

After crushing and the removal of the stalks, the grapes are pumped into chambers above the modern hydraulic presses, and the juice is allowed to run into collecting sumps, while the stalks, skins, and pips are consigned to the presses that at once operate a second pressing. The must is pumped from the sumps into *tinajas* – that is, fermenting-pots (in the big bodegas they are made from cement, but in most of the small ones the old clay pots are still used); and there they lie in symmetrical and attractive rows. They each hold between 6,000 and 7,000 litres of must, and, in a large bodega like Alvear, there are sometimes more than a hundred pots. The pots are left without lids at this stage while fermentation is developing, and every stage can be seen and examined, from the newly poured must to the wine that has achieved its first boisterous fermentation. This is extremely interesting to watch, the liquid apparently boiling, with bubbles breaking and the whole liquid appearing to seethe. It also looks extremely unpleasant, rather like water from the River Thames; and yet in a few weeks it will clear and the wine become like crystal.

The wine is left in the fermenting-pots for two months after fermentation stops. The first fermentation takes between fifteen days and a month, and then follows the secondary fermentation, without disturbing the wine, while it clarifies completely. It is then piped off into butts, for removal to the bodega so that it can be blended and take its place in the appropriate solera. It is in this process that the vinification differs from that of Jerez, where, up to now, the must is fermented in the butt and not in pots or vats; but I am told that more than one of the great Jerez bodegas are changing over to the pot system. Certainly it would be difficult to find a better wine than that made in Montilla by the pot system, and indeed it is said that the old clay pots do contribute to the quality of the wine; but this may come under the heading of old wives' tales. The modern cement vats appear to produce wine of equal quality. As in Jerez, the wine develops in the oak butts and produces the yeasts that form the 'flower', which appears in the spring and autumn. This we have discussed in the last chapter.

Montilla can be, and often is, sold a year old, and this is the common wine of the country, the *vino corriente de Montilla*, although in no way to be confused with a *vino de mesa* (which it is not). Most of the wine, however, is sent to its appropriate solera, where it goes through the usual process, emerging as a *fino*, an *amontillado*, or an *oloroso*. Before bottling, the special wines are clarified with beaten white of egg, and in some bodegas the vintagers are said to add a pinch of earth brought from Lebrija in Seville, which is supposed to have a special property for clarifying wine very quickly. I cannot find the truth of this; it may be a local ritual. Or maybe it doesn't happen at all. But I like the idea of it.

In the large and small bodegas of Córdoba and Montilla, the whole business of making up the soleras, blending, and finally bottling and distribution is carried on. I saw two of these. One was comparatively small; it belonged to Señor Antonio Alarcón, who is justly proud of the excellent wine he produces in most grades. He is especially proud of an *oloroso* that comes from a hundred-year-old solera. It would indeed be difficult to fault. After dinner I was taken over his bodega and through the Arabian Nights streets of old Córdoba. We tasted wines until nearly two in the morning – which was about the latest I had ever looked at wine with a critical eye. However, dinner had been light and late, so I thoroughly enjoyed the selection of wines from *finos* to *olorosos*, which were all excellent of their type.

The next day in Córdoba I visited a very large bodega belonging to Señor Carbonell. When his family bought it a hundred years ago, it was the oldest bodega in Córdoba, and it had some correspondingly interesting soleras. Those great bodega naves, with hundreds of butts in treble rows, are indeed a sight; they always amaze me, despite the many occasions on which I have seen them. From a barrel somewhere in the middle of the solera, using the same method as in Jerez, were taken samples, first, of a *fino* that I judged to be at about its best; next, of a twenty-year-old *fino*, now of course an *amontillado*, that was a pale golden brown and, I was delighted to see, still retained that green glint which I have come to look for. This was followed by a collection of four soleras from the four oldest butts in the bodega. Five years were assumed to have passed between each two, and the youngest was about a hundred years old. They were naturally very dark, and I couldn't find any green; but then there is very little green in any of us at that great age. There were slight variations in the taste. All, however, were uniformly dry and very good indeed.

After making the acquaintance of these very old gentlemen, I was given a glass of the Pedro Ximénez that every bodega apparently likes to trot out at the very end to ruin the taste of those that have gone before. They are always superb of their kind, as this was. But, without being ungracious, I cannot help wishing bodegas wouldn't do it.

I should mention that this one has the happy idea of complimenting visitors by asking them to write in chalk on the end of a butt of wine in one of the soleras, instead of in the more customary visitors' book. You see the usual appropriate remarks – with the usual inanities too, I fear – in every language under the sun.

Montilla and Moriles wines are grouped officially into four classes.

Finos	These have an alcoholic content of not less than 16° to 16½° after fermentation, with an acidity of less than 0·60.
Finos viejos	Corresponding to the Jerez *amontillado*, these have a degree of alcohol from 17° to 17½°. Again the acidity is less than 0·60.
Olorosos	In Montilla, these are called strong-scented wines, which indeed they are, of 18° or 19° alcohol and with a volatile acidity of less than 0·70.
Olorosos viejos	These come from the oldest bodegas and go as high as 19° to 21° alcohol, with a volatile acidity of not more than 0·70.

Some of the large bodegas in Córdoba distil their own brandy, which I found rather sweeter than the Jerez brandies; I am told that there is a lively export trade with Italy, as they have become popular through the predilection for them of the American armed forces in Spain, who have now spread this rather apocryphal gospel abroad. They also make a highly interesting punch or *ponche*, a mixture of brandy and fermented fruit juices, called 'Seductor' – and it might well be used as one. It is presented in what appears to be a solid silver bottle; actually it is a glass bottle completely covered in silver paper, with a nice little red tassel at the top, and it is reputed to have a considerable vogue in South American countries. I tasted it, but I cannot for the moment think of an appropriate way of describing in detail this potent and interesting concoction.

CHAPTER 4

The Wines of the Rioja

The Rioja, like all Gaul, is divided into three parts – and, like Gaul, it produces excellent wines. The Rioja district is partly in the provinces of Burgos, Alava, and Navarre and comprises the whole of Logroño. It starts a few miles to the east of Miranda de Ebro on the main San Sebastián to Burgos road, and it stretches as far as Alfaro about eighty miles to the west. Vines are grown and wine is made all over this wonderfully beautiful land of gentle hills, many capped with castles, villages, and churches, and surrounded by the mountains of the Sierra de Cantabria in the north, which your local grower will tell you is the great protector of the Rioja vines, giving them shelter from the bleak winds of winter. This land, through which the Ebro flows from beginning to end, is in my opinion one of the most beautiful vine-growing areas in the world; even without its superlative wines, it would be well worth a visit for any tourist with an eye for scenery. I am writing this as I sit on the balcony of my room in the Conde de Haro Hotel at Haro, overlooking this altogether wonderful landscape, with the poplar-lined Ebro quietly flowing a hundred yards or so below, and with patches of vines growing everywhere within sight until they reach the higher slopes of the sierra.

Wines have been made in the Rioja, as in most places in Spain, from time immemorial, but there is a particular history attached to these particularly good wines, mainly because of their special excellence and the fact that they have been much sought after by the kings and

56

Plate 5. A cellar in Rioja
Subsecretaría de Turismo, Madrid

grandees of Spain, who would obviously go to some trouble to provide themselves with the best wine, even though transport might be difficult. This region is roughly at the meeting-place of Aragon, Navarre, and Castile; it was therefore easily accessible for those kingdoms and provided indeed their *vino corriente*. Just exactly what happened to the vineyards under the Moors is not recorded; but, as elsewhere in Spain, there are records that the Prophet was disobeyed in his tenet that proscribes wine for the Faithful, so we must suppose that wine went on being made here in Rioja. Certainly, in the sixteenth and seventeenth centuries, the wines had become world-famous, but long before that, in 1102, King Sancho of Navarre founded a monastery in the Rioja, and its vineyards were specially mentioned in the deeds.

It is interesting that even in the sixteenth century the imitation of wine, or the stealing of the good name to put on an inferior wine (a practice that is certainly not in disuse today), was pretty well established, and the Riojans in 1560 adopted what must have been one of the first trade-marks ever made, so that they could mark their casks and institute their own *denominación de origen*. They designed an odd kind of anagram (shown on page 88), and the first trade association of wine-growers in Spain was founded thereby. In 1635 the authorities in Logroño made an order against any kind of cart traffic on certain streets, as the rumbling shook the must in the cellars below and harmed the ageing of the wines (but I think there must be something more to it than this; it hardly sounds possible), while in 1655 the Vicar-General of the Diocese is reported to have excommunicated the Municipal Council for harvesting their wines without observing the rules that had been laid down to regulate the vintage. This again sounds apocryphal.

Rioja is to Spain more or less what the Bordeaux vineyards are to France; it produces wine by the same methods, and with sometimes nearly as much care. It is a distinctive wine on its own merit and makes no claim to be otherwise, but it owes much of its technique and know-how to the French *vignerons*. When the phylloxera scourge hit France in the late nineteenth century and partly wiped out its vineyards, many of the French *vignerons* came to the Rioja, which is reasonably near, and bought or rented vineyards and made wine that they blended with

D

what they could find of their own, to maintain their trade, although those years were very bad indeed for them. With them they brought French techniques, which, when added to the centuries-old Spanish methods, improved the wine a great deal. These methods are now the traditional methods of wine-making in the Rioja area, and certainly the vine is cultivated and the wine made with some care, and indeed with love.

Later, when the French vineyards had been replanted after the phylloxera with immune American vine-stocks, the phylloxera crossed the Pyrenees, probably with one of the French *vignerons* whose business Rioja had saved. At the same time it appeared in the south of Spain through Gibraltar, which no doubt the Spanish put down to one of the little tricks of perfidious Albion. The scourge came up from the south and down from the north, wiping out numerous areas of vines in the same way as it had in France, although, for some reason or other, part of the Valdepeñas area was spared, and there are still pre-phylloxera vines growing there. These were years, I am told, of tremendous hardship throughout the vineyards of Spain; but eventually the phylloxera-immune stocks were imported and planted, and the wine is better than ever. Although it is often claimed in France that the pre-phylloxera wine was best, few of my generation and those younger will ever know the truth. Certain it is, however, that the fine wines made today are of superb quality, as they are indeed in the Rioja.

Having already said much in praise of the wines of Spain (and I hope to say a good deal more before this book is finished), I doubt whether Spain will ever produce really *great* wine. Good wine certainly, fine wine often in the Rioja and in one or two pockets of viniculture; but the great wines of France are bred on soils such as Spain does not possess, and made by techniques that are foreign to the Spanish nature, and in a climate very different from that which exists only a comparatively few miles away across the Pyrenees. The great wines of France are uniformly produced from grapes (usually of a single variety) grown in pockets of gravelly, stony soil, where they are gathered and made into wine under the direction of a single *vigneron* and marketed by him under his own name and that of his *château*. They may be produced, as most of them are, by a time-honoured process of fermentation, ageing and racking and ageing in cask, and sold as the completely authentic wine of a certain very limited area and of a given year, bottled at exactly the right time in the place where it was made. Thus, if the wines are kept properly and the year is a good one, they will be brought to the table in as perfect a condition as they possibly can be, given their age. They may be drunk too young or too old, but the wine at least started its life with a good birth certificate.

Nothing comparable to this exists in Spain. The wine is universally made, usually in the bodega of the shipper, but from grapes bought from great numbers of little growers, and sometimes from wine bought from a cooperative, or made by a small grower, and blended to form a standard type of wine. In the Rioja, for instance, the vines are grown by small farmers, with an average of between two and five hectares of land, who tend to grow the kind of grape they like best. Thus, while certain strains of grape are popular and certainly go well with similar grapes, there is no consistency; the art is in the blending rather than the cultivation of a specific grape made in a given year and sold. I have been talking, of course, about the fine wines of Bordeaux and the Côte d'Or, for most of the ordinary wines in France are made on much the same principle as the Spanish.

There is, however, one big difference: throughout Spain *chaptalisation*, or the addition of sugar to the wine in fermentation, is unknown, while, although not practised (much) in Bordeaux, it is greatly practised in other parts of France. In Spain a certain amount of *mistela*, or unfermented must, which is very sweet, is kept for blending some types of wine. Again, a certain proportion of the old wines in the Rioja area are kept as a reserve for blending, and this is why you find the words 'Reserva' or 'Gran Reserva' on standard wine labels, which simply means that these comparatively old, matured wines are used for blending table wines in a very modified way, as they are used universally in the Sherry country of Jerez.

The climate of the Rioja is fairly stable and is altogether suitable for viniculture. The winters, although cold, are seldom terribly severe, and the rains are usually consistent in the rainy season; the summers are very hot, but rain falls occasionally, and this makes for excellent wine. Sometimes there is a disastrous year, like 1959, when it rained all the time, and the grapes arrived mildewed at the bodegas, and most of the wine went for vinegar. Indeed, it was worth very little more.

The soil varies according to the three parts of the Rioja, but it is chalky in its general formation and not particularly rich. This, again, makes for good wine. The three parts of the Rioja are the Rioja Alta, which is to the west and is centred on Haro – here are produced fine wines of a not very high alcoholic content, never more than 14°, and usually about 12°; the Rioja Baja, where the bodegas are centred on Logroño and the villages around it, which produce again a fine wine but of a higher alcoholic strength, without quite the breeding of the Rioja Alta; and the third, much smaller district, which is contained in the two pockets to the north of the river Ebro near Haro and is called the Rioja Alavesa – this produces a slight variation in the wine, which is different from the others in that it has a certain smoothness; this I found very attractive.

Generally speaking, the Riojan tradition is to make wines by the Bordeaux method; that is to say, the wine is fermented in great oak vats, where it undergoes its first tumultuous fermentation in about ten to twelve days, after which it is either racked off into storage-vats, also mostly of oak, or passed directly into the barrel, where it undergoes its second fermentation, to be racked by moving the wine from one cask to another three times in the first year. It is then clarified and put into the ageing barrels, being racked perhaps once a year; after two or three years it is ready for bottling or being sold in bulk. After bottling it is binned for six months or so, or as long as it is required before selling.

The great bodegas of Haro – where there are no fewer than twelve large bodegas that export wines, besides many smaller ones – are indeed imposing, with endless great buildings containing literally thousands of hogsheads of wine in five tiered rows. Ageing of the wine is considered of great importance in the Rioja; even the white wines are sometimes kept for four or five years before being bottled, and many of them for much longer. Most of the bodegas show with great pride this *reserva* wine, and many of them too have their private cellars of bottled wines, which they do not sell but produce for the interested visitor. And very good they are.

I think it is necessary to say something about the years that are printed on the labels, which are not always strictly accurate. It is perfectly true that there are casks of very, very old wine in the Rioja of a given year, and I have myself seen and tasted wines of 1904, 1910, and later that are indeed authentic of those years. On the other hand, we must remember that a modified solera system operates with table wines, and it may mean only that the wine has been made with a proportion of the old wine from that year added. Then again, it may sometimes happen that one bodega has had a big success with a wine of a certain year, such as 'Gran Reserva 1928', and this has tended to establish itself as a *marque* rather than a mere matter of fact. The 'Gran Reserva 1928' I was given to taste was actually about fifteen years old, and probably all the better for it, but the bodega-owner thought it the most natural thing in the world to keep his *marque*. Furthermore, the year in which the wine has been made is not by any means of so much significance as it is in France, because the climate is very much more consistent, and the wines of one year, with certain exceptions like 1959, do not vary a great deal. What is important is the age of the wine, because the Rioja wines do age tremendously well, both in cask and in bottle, and there is a very big difference between a young wine, three or four years old, and the older wines in which the great bodegas take such pride.

Apart from the wines in the Rioja that are made by the great bodegas, some of them world-famous names, wine is also made in village co-operatives, which produce a *corriente* wine of superb quality for what it is, and by a diminishing number of small growers who may buy the grapes of their neighbours but who make the wine themselves, usually to sell to the big bodegas, or sometimes to their own private trade customers, always in Spain. The wine may be made, in the case of the big bodegas, and certainly of the two cooperatives that I have seen, by the most modern methods and in very large quantities indeed; and, while there is nothing in Rioja to match the stainless steel splendour of

Château Latour, some of the bodegas have very good and efficient systems of tile-lined cement vats and similar modern fittings. The small bodega has none of this, and I am rather glad to say that many of the larger bodegas still retain their faith in the oak vats. All, however, age their wine in cask, with the exception of the cooperatives, where the wine must be sold and cleared within two years of being made.

I stayed for some days in the Rioja and visited many of the bodegas, large and small. These I shall describe – for, as in France, the wine varied from one to another. I have tasted excellent wine, indeed very excellent wine, from those bodegas that keep the traditional system of cobwebby oak vats and barrels, and I have had excellent wine from more modern installations. I do not think it would be fair to make a distinction on this point; after all, it can well be argued that, if super-modern methods can be used in Château Latour, which is generally agreed to have produced the best wine of the Médoc in 1964, certainly there can be nothing against it. I suppose I just happen to like cobwebs in wine-cellars.

Most of the bodegas produce two qualities of wine; the first and best I suppose we can term the export quality, although far more of it is sold in Spain than elsewhere, and it is to be found universally throughout Spain on the wine list of every good restaurant and hotel. They also make for their national consumption wine that is usually sold in bulk, and again it is of very good quality, but I have the impression that most of the *corriente* wines of the Rioja come from the cooperatives. The wines, whether they are sold in England or in Spanish restaurants, are cheap; and this is true throughout Spain, although unfortunately the big hotels and restaurants will not serve the *corriente* wines – especially the enormous number of large hotels that have sprung up all along the Mediterranean coast. While I suppose that most holiday-makers are prepared to spend a bit more for their wine when they are abroad, I for one deplore the fact that you cannot have an occasional good *corriente*, which in Spain is usually very drinkable indeed, especially if it comes from Rioja, and very much cheaper.

The large bodegas nearly all produce a range of about three *tintos*, which are classed rather by age than by anything else, starting with a wine of four years old, and another one of perhaps six years, and a *reserva*, which may be ten or fifteen years old. It is the *tintos* of the Rioja that are its chief glory. Then again, they will produce a dry white and a *semiseco* and a somewhat sweeter white wine and, of course, the inevitable *rosado* to take care of the growing market for this now popular wine, so delicious on a hot summer day when it is served really cold. This constitutes the main difference between the French and Spanish types of wine-production; in Spain most districts make wine of several types, whereas, in France, Médoc wines come from Médoc, Graves from Graves, wines of Burgundy from the Côte d'Or, and the Beaujolais (some of them) from Beaujolais. It is possible and, I think, very probable that a good many of the French wines from all these districts have some Spanish blood in their veins, and indeed they are none the worse for it, since, in the Rioja as in most other districts of Spain, the wine is perfectly honest, both in its essential character and its alcoholic strength, which qualities make it very suitable for blending – and I can think of some wines from outside Spain that could be improved by an infusion of good Spanish wine.

In all the great bodegas in Haro that I had the pleasure of visiting, I found a wide variety of wine; where popular demand from England and elsewhere had not tended to alter the basic style of the wine, they were universally good. Most of the bodegas have their special pride and joy in the wines that they, no doubt rightly, consider they make better than anybody else, as (for instance) Bodegas 'Rioja' Santiago, who make their wine, and market it in square bottles, under the *marque* 'Yago'. This method of bottling, which they have been using for fifteen years, makes for easy storage (obviously square bottles are much easier to bin than round ones, and they also save a great deal of space); it is, I am told, being adopted by the German wine trade, and I was able to give this very unpalatable piece of information to Señor Don Angel Santiago, who had clapped a patent on his form of bottling – he was, to say the least of it, disconcerted to know that it was no longer all his own. I suspect that he went off to consult his lawyers, but I doubt whether he will have much luck, because every kind of bottle has been made at some time or other in the long history of wine-making. The bottle is quite attractive, rather like a square hock bottle, tapering off into an ordinary round neck, but of course it has nothing whatever to do with the wine inside. Señor Santiago makes his wine from grapes from the Rioja Alta and also the Rioja Alavesa. He makes the wine in his bodega at Labastida, a village about seven kilometres from Haro.

In passing, I should mention that the word *bodega* is the same whether the wine is made there or merely stored, blended, and bottled there, in contradistinction to the French *pressoire* for the place where the grapes are pressed and fermented and the *chais* where the wine is stored and aged. In Spain, the bodega where the wine is made is called a *bodega de elaboración*; the Spanish equivalent of *chais* is *bodega de crianza*. Señor Santiago's *bodega de elaboración* was then being scoured out ready for the vintage that was due to begin in about a fortnight.

The wines of which Don Angel is most proud are his old red wines called 'Rioja Santiago', of which he has really enormous stocks, and he is especially proud of a genuine 1949, which is a very good wine indeed, but with, I think, rather a dry aftertaste; this may have been due, in the bottle that was opened for me, to a little too much tannin, but the wine has great character. His white wines, which are well aged and never sold until after four years, are pale golden and are perfectly fresh and lively. He was kind enough to open for me a bottle of white wine; the label was printed with the mystic number 1908. But this, with the best will in the world, I cannot take too seriously. The wine, although very mellow and quite delicious, showed no trace of age at all, except for a suspicion of woodiness, which might perhaps be due to the sulphur with which all the white-wine casks are prepared, as they are everywhere else. His great pride, however, is a wonderful bin of 1904 red wine, which is never sold – and I don't blame him. It was a great privilege to drink it, and an even greater privilege to be given a bottle to take away. This wine is truly remarkable, and, had I been given it in a decanter without any knowledge of its origin, I should have been hard pressed to say whence it came. It was perhaps the finest of the Spanish wines that I have drunk.

The Bodegas Bilbainas are the biggest in the Rioja, and, in the absence of the present managing director, I was shown round by the

Plate 6. The glorious Rioja: a vineyard near Haro

Kenneth Swain

previous head of the firm, who has now retired after fifty-one years in Haro and Valdepeñas, where they have another large bodega. This bodega in Haro is truly enormous, and it was a great pleasure and relief when, having been shown with justifiable pride every operation, from the making of casks and the hammering together of the wooden boxes in which the wine is exported, backwards to the actual making of the wine, I found myself seated comfortably in the office of Señor Don Santiago de Ugarte with a bottle of his best sparkling wine opened for the occasion.

This bodega is the only one in the Rioja to make sparkling wine by the *méthode champenoise*. The owners are quite justifiably proud in this division of the business; although relatively small, it compares favourably with some of the *cavas* in Panadés and certainly with any of the bodegas that make Spanish sparkling wines by other methods. The quality is exceptionally good, and, while (in common with all other Spanish sparkling wine) it is not comparable in actual taste with true Champagne, it is an excellent wine. It has generally a softer taste, but it is well made, and the *brut* is very dry indeed, with a liqueur addition of less than 1 per cent. The Bodegas Bilbainas have some vineyards of their own adjoining the bodega, and their grapes, the Garnacha Blanca (which are comparatively small, white grapes, not over-sweet), are considered to be especially suitable for the making of sparkling wine; the producers reckon to have them out of the way before the normal Riojan vintage starts. Three great presses work on them. The first fermentation is carried out in oak vats, and the wine is transferred immediately into the cask for the secondary fermentation, after which it is clarified, blended, and bottled with its temporary corks. It then starts on its long period of ageing in a horizontal position, before the penultimate stage of being put in racks at an angle of 45°, with its daily shake-up; and so after six months into the upside-down vertical position before being finished. The sparkling wine is usually sold in about five to seven years.

Owing to the complexity of the export market, this bodega makes a great many wines, both red and white – about ten *tintos* and eight *blancos* in qualities and prices to suit most demands throughout the world. I tasted a good many of them; the best seemed to be the 'Viña Pomal', which is an excellent *tinto* of some age, and the 'Cepa de Oro', which is a pale gold, and the 'Viña Paceta'. It also makes a sweet white wine called 'Brillante'. This is certainly brilliant to look at, and it is much beloved by the tourist trade, but in my opinion it appears to have lost character to sweetness. It is difficult to describe this truly enormous bodega. Like Topsy, it 'just growed', and now every nook and cranny is filled with wine – wine in tanks, wine in barrels, wine in bottles. Vast quantities of wine can be seen, most of it growing deliciously older every day.

At the medium-sized bodega of R. López de Heredia, Viña Tondonia, S.A., oak is considered to be the only material in which wine should be contained, apart from bottles. Here again the great presses were being made ready, and everything was being cleaned and furbished, but all the fermenting-vats – and some of them were huge, containing 40,000 to 50,000 litres – were of oak; the whole process of first and second fermentation is carried out in the casks. Señor Don Pedro López de Heredia is an enthusiast and a great believer in wood; his wines have all the character you would expect from their being carefully made and long matured. The house of Tondonia, founded in 1877, makes four white wines, five reds, and a *rosado*. The white wines, which vary from a *semidulce* wine called 'Viña Zaconia' to a very dry wine called 'Viña Tondonia', are excellent. 'Viña Tondonia' *blanco* is bottled from the wood after six years; it has a good nose, is splendidly golden, and is quite delicious. The red wines are all excellent, strong, full-bodied wines with a good nose, and they vary from the 'Rioja Clarete Fino', which is bottled after three years in wood, to the 'Viña Tondonia' *tinto*, which has had six years in barrel and is a wonderful dark red and quite exceptional.

The pride and joy of this bodega is the private cellar, which contains a hundred or more bins of the wines that have been made over the last fifty years or so. The wine of every year is not present, and, when I asked if they had any wine of my year (which is 1905), they regretted very much that they could offer me only 1904 or 1906. This great private cellar is most impressive. In its centre is a round table, made from the bottom of an immense fermenting-vat and standing on barrels, at which you sit and taste the wine. I was given a dry white wine of 1938, which certainly had lost none of its body and was not appreciably darker than the four- or six-year-old wines of the same breed that I also tasted. Moreover I was given a 'Viña Tondonia' 1934, which was brilliant in colour and had a lovely nose and a great deal of character; if I had to choose between a Bordeaux of 1934, which is considered by some to be a good year, and this particular wine, I would choose the Rioja. This splendid and altogether remarkable cellar of very fine wines is dubbed colloquially the *cementerio* (cemetery) – and not inappropriately, since paradise is usually entered that way. Behind oak doors are wines from the foundation of the bodega in 1877; but the head of the firm was away, and he had very wisely taken the key with him.

It was in the process of being interred, or rather pickled, in the cemetery that I discovered the origin of the slender silver or gold chicken wire with which the best Spanish wine is always enmeshed. I have often wondered about this because, while pretty, it seemed to perform no useful function whatever; but, upon mentioning this fact, I was told that it was in the first place a very sensible idea. The best wines, as in other parts of the world, were imitated by unscrupulous wine-merchants who were not above forging a label or two; and so, to ensure the integrity of the wine in the bottle, a few of the best shippers encased their bottles in this charming wire and sealed it off at the bottom with the private seal of their own bodega. This they thought would make their wine less vulnerable to imitation. In consequence everybody else started to do exactly the same thing; the seals are no longer used, but the wire remains as an embellishment and as a kind of outward and visible sign that the wine within has an inward and spiritual grace that requires protection.

Some very good wines are made at the Compañía Vinícola del Norte de España, again a large bodega. It is the second largest in Haro, and I have long known it for the good wine that is marketed under the name of C.V.N.E. The wines are made by comparatively modern methods (the ageing in wood is taken for granted in the Rioja for all fine wines) from grapes of both Rioja Alavesa and the Rioja Alta, and they have a smoothness that I found excellent; in fact, the best of them are very fine wines indeed. Their *blanco-seco* is called 'Monopole'; it is dry, fragrant, and comparable with the wines grown in countries further north. But I suppose their chief pride is in their three main types of red wine: the 'Corona', which is their younger wine (that is, about four years old); the 'Imperial Gran Reserva', which bears the date 1949; and the 'Viña Real Oro'. This last wine is extremely smooth – a completely natural, clean wine with none of the dry aftertaste that is typical of most Riojan wines. I found it very, very good indeed. It is not surprising that on the wine list of the local restaurant in Haro this particular wine is by far the most expensive, although the list, naturally enough, includes all the best *marques* of Rioja. It is extremely expensive by Spanish standards, and very cheap for its quality by any other; but I can well understand that it should fetch, as it deserves to fetch, a good price.

The restaurant I have mentioned, called 'El Terete', is worth a note because, among those I know, it is the only one that you enter through a butcher's shop. You go upstairs to tables and benches of pine scrubbed to an immaculate white; the food there is first class by any international standards. You order from the menu, and the waiters pop down and cut the meat off the joint in the shop downstairs. In passing, besides their baby lamb, I can recommend their *alubias* – a delicious bean soup, made from butter beans, the only trouble being that one eats too much of it to enjoy the baby lamb to follow.

The fine wines of the bodega Federico Paternina are well known all over the world. Naturally they have a very big export trade, and the stacks of wooden cases ready for shipment can be seen to be going to the uttermost corners of the earth. The bodega's best known wine is the *tinto* 'Banda Azul', which, I suppose, would be about four years old and is uniformly good; but it has another wine called 'Viña Vial' – an excellent wine of about ten years – and also a real giant of a wine, 'Gran Reserva', some bottles having a label calling it 1928, though I don't think I could vouch for the validity of this age, and I must say that my hosts seemed rather surprised that they should be asked to do so. On the other hand, the wine itself has the dignity of a wine of great age, and I have no doubt at all that there is in it some very old wine somewhere along the line. It can certainly be recommended as a big wine with lots of character and with not too much dryness in the after-taste. Federico Paternina also make some excellent white wines, although their 'Monte Haro' is *dulce* – too *dulce* for me. They have a good *blanco seco* that is a very good example of a fine white Rioja wine, and another wine rejoicing in the name of 'Rinsol', which is a good deal better than the name sounds.

My mentor in some of these expeditions was Señor Don Antonio Larrea, the local official representative of the Consejo Regulador de la Denominación de Origen Rioja (the Spanish equivalent of the French *appellation contrôlée* authority), who was unprejudiced in his views. I also found him uniformly courteous and interested in all that I was trying to do and say. Under his guidance I visited one of the largest cooperatives in the Rioja, at San Vicente de la Sonsierra, an altogether charming village perhaps fourteen kilometres from Haro, with the tiled houses rising on the little hill crowned by a castle and a church in the best Spanish tradition.

The vintage had not yet begun, but this quite vast factory – and I am aware that this is an unkind word to use, for a place that makes nearly 5,000,000 litres of good wine a year – is really the last word in a *bodega de elaboración* for the mass-production of *corriente* wine. It is a perfectly straightforward operation; the grapes are brought in by the farmers, the machinery for removing the stalks and so on is absolutely modern, there are four great presses for the second pressing, and the *mosto* is pumped into row upon row of fermenting-vats in three tiers. The bodega is built on the side of the hill, so that each storey of vats has its own entrance. After the first fermentation of ten to twelve days, the wine is pumped into the second range of storage-vats, and it is ready to drink in the year following. Most of it is sold in the second year; indeed, it all has to be cleared by then because the vats are needed. I was told that there is never any difficulty in selling the output from this extremely well-run cooperative, and I was given the wine to taste directly from four of the storage tanks. There was a slight variation; this might well be expected, because they use more than one kind of grape, but, considering that this wine is sold in the wine-shops at about eight to ten pesetas a litre, it was quite excellent, clean and a rich ruby colour, but not too dark and with quite a good nose. If I never had anything else but this *vino corriente* to drink for the rest of my life, I should come to no harm at all. When I consider the *ordinaires* that I have had to put up with at one time or another in various places around the world, I find myself full of admiration for these very honest, decent wines.

On a morning in very early October I slipped out on to my balcony at the Hotel Conde de Haro, to find the valley of the Ebro below me shrouded in mist, with the low hills, topped by their castles, villages, and churches, rising out of a white sea like islands, and with the vineyards draping the slopes and the mountains behind in the early morning sun. It was indescribably beautiful, like an old Japanese print. Soon the mists disappeared, and my courteous guide arrived to take me to see a bodega or two that he thought would be of special interest.

First of all we visited the Bodegas Riojanas in Cenicero (which means 'ash-tray'), where they appear to be not unreasonably proud of the wine they make, which is exported in really enormous quantities to almost every part of the world except England. This Señor Marcelo Frias regretted; but, as he sold without difficulty all of his excellent wine, he did not consider it a major problem. The wines in his bodega seemed to be universally good. A mixture of the grapes from the Rioja Alta and the Rioja Alavesa is used, and the wines are made, as far as the *tintos* are concerned, from the Garnacha, Tempranillo, and Graciano varieties, and from the Malvasía and Viura for the *blancos*. Señor Frias has considerable vineyards of his own, and he also buys other carefully selected grapes from local farmers. His wines are made entirely in wood (he will not have anything in stainless steel or cement near the place), and they undergo the first fermentation in vats holding 20,000 to 40,000 litres. They receive their secondary fermentation in wood, and then they go through the process of being racked three times in the first year, twice in the second, and once in the third; after which some are sold, and the others are kept for sale later and possibly put into a *reserva*.

The most important wines of the Bodegas Riojanas are the 'Monte

Real' and the 'Viña Albina' as regards *tintos*; I was given both the six-year-old wines, and a bottle was opened of the 'Viña Albina 1942 Reserva'. The 'Viña Albina' is the drier of the two, but both wines are full-bodied and a dark ruby in colour. All these wines were first class, especially the 1942, which I was assured belonged honestly to that year – and I believe it. This bodega makes several white wines, but the most attractive I found to be the *marque* called 'Medieval', which is sold at about three years old and is a very pale wine for a Rioja, very dry, with a good nose, and altogether acceptable and comparable with white wines anywhere, other than the classic vintages.

Courteous farewells were made, and we were on our way to Elciego a few kilometres away; but the barriers over the level-crossing were down, and my mentor groaned, 'Why are the barriers always down at Cenicero? I have never yet known them to be up'.

There was a goods train in the siding in Cenicero station, with steam up and facing our way. After a quarter of an hour or so a whistling was heard a long way down the line, and the Bilbao–Logroño express came in sight along the single track, stopping a couple of hundred yards from the goods train and whistling for a signal. Nothing happened for some time, while the two engines whistled at each other intermittently, each obviously trying to stare the other out. Meanwhile the barriers remained resolutely down, and we could see an argument proceeding on the station platform a little distance away. More whistles – and no hope that the two engines were any nearer an agreement than the United Nations. So I did the only sensible thing. I descended from the car and, gathering some grapes from the adjoining vineyard of Bodegas Riojanas, spent an agreeable quarter of an hour watching or rather listening to the two trains arguing the toss and waiting for the barrier to go up. After which I decided I would take a constitutional along the road and leave the car to pick me up, which it did another quarter of an hour and one kilometre later. I gather that the express triumphed, even though the goods train had received reinforcements from somewhere else in the form of another train – and so I spent three-quarters of an hour quite pleasantly in the middle of a lovely country.

Just outside the ancient little walled town of Laguardia are the

Bodegas Palacio. Here they make a great deal of excellent quality wine and more *mosto*, which is not one of my favourite drinks. Nevertheless it has apparently an increasing trade, both domestic and for export. The grapes are crushed and the must extracted in exactly the same way as for wine, but fermentation is stopped by refrigeration, and the resulting grape-juice is filtered and sold as a delicious, natural sweet drink in vast quantities – millions of litres from the Bodegas Palacio alone.

The wine made here is all from the grapes of the Rioja Alavesa, and entirely from their own vineyards and those of their employees who have a few vines of their own; and this is very unusual. These grapes are exclusively used for the making of wine, while the brought-in grapes are made into *mosto*. The company owns something like a hundred hectares of vines, which – under the new system of cultivation, using tractors instead of mules – maintain much fewer vines per hectare than they used to do. In the old days, 2,500 to 3,000 vines to the hectare was quite usual, and now it is between 1,500 and 2,000. These vines will produce two to three kilos of grapes in an average year, and twenty-three kilos of grapes will make one quintale or sixteen litres of wine, so if you are good at arithmetic you can work out how much wine this very well run company of bodegas can make.

Here delicious *entremeses* were spread out on a table in the shade, and a bottle of thirty-year-old wine and other wines laid out for tasting. The *marques* of which they feel particularly proud are, as regards white wines, 'Regio', which is sweet and contains Moscatel grapes, though not too many (I found the wine very clean and attractive and by no means cloying to the palate), and 'Semillon', which has nothing to do with the grape of that name and is an extremely dry white wine, by all means to be recommended. The red wines are the 'Glorioso' – a clean, light wine with a faint, rather fragrant nose and a light colour; and their 'Reserva Especial', which is the same wine only older. Both the white and the red wines are of about 12° to 12½° alcohol. I was given to drink two wines from the private cellar, a *vino blanco seco*, of the same quality as the 'Semillon', that was thirty years old, and had been twenty-five years in bottle. This wine was very little darker than the

three-year-old wine I had just tasted; it was dry and full-bodied, with a faintly *maderisé* nose, and a first-class wine, but how I longed for that little touch of magic one finds in a Montrachet of good lineage! But it was not there. And yet I am continually surprised at the great age to which these white wines of the Rioja live. To match this beautiful white wine, an equally old bottle (exact age unknown) of the 'Reserva Especial' was produced. In this case there was little of the dry after-taste, and the wine was darker, absolutely clean, and old beyond question, but with no sign of decay or deterioration.

A few hundred yards up the road from the Bodegas Palacio, you leave the car and enter this old walled hill town, once a favourite resort of the medieval kings of Navarre, and now, with Venice, one of the few places remaining on this earth where the motor-car is not allowed to enter. The vines encircle the hill and come up to the walls; inside, the only sound, apart from the cheerful chattering of children, is the rumbling of the wine-casks as they are trundled through the narrow, balconied streets and through one of the six main gates of the town to the waiting *camiones*. One can walk right round the walls, and the view from almost any part, and especially from the little bandstand to the north, is absolutely marvellous. Everywhere the vineyards spread over the low hill, but never more than a hectare or so before the vines are intermixed with other crops.

The kings of Navarre maintained a castle here, and, although all that remains is a twelfth-century tower, which is now being restored, there are many of the large houses or small palaces where their court used to live. Laguardia is entirely devoted to wine; it reminds me of that other walled town of about the same size, Riquewihr in Alsace, where the whole town is occupied in wine-making; but you can drive around Riquewihr, and it has lost much of its charm thereby, wonderful though it is. In Laguardia none of this happens. As you walk through the narrow streets, you can see, about six inches from the bottom of every house, or at least every other one, a little hole in the wall; it is through this little hole that the wine is pumped up from the vats in the bodegas, where they were cut in the solid rock under the town, into the casks before being trundled out through the gates to the waiting trucks.

E

I entered one of these bodegas under a house, passing first through a medieval iron-studded door into a small patio with patterned cobbles, very redolent of the mule that undoubtedly quartered there at night, and then deep down into the bodega itself. There, in two long narrow cellars, I counted twelve enormous barrel-shaped vats, each holding 5,000 litres. These huge vats are of such a size that they could quite obviously not be brought in through the door and down the steep stairs; they must have been brought in stave by stave and hoop by hoop and coopered in the actual bodega. Once in position they will make wine for a few hundred years. But even here, in this little bodega in Laguardia, the owner has his private *cementerio* at the end of the cellar, where he keeps half a dozen or so bottles of the wine of each year; they go back quite a long way, and I expect they are kept for the three great occasions – births, marriages, and deaths.

Here the general practice is to tread the grapes as they have been trodden for the last thousand years or more; and, while I was unfortunate in that the vintage had not yet started, the vats were ready and the *comportas* had been washed and everything was being prepared for the harvest. These dim bodegas, with their wealth of good wine, have to be seen to be believed. I am told that the whole hill is honeycombed with them, and certainly, in this little town, where there is no danger of being run down by a car or having one's nerves shattered by the roar of an unsilenced motor-scooter, I can conceive that some remains of tranquillity in life may be preserved here for a little time yet.

The wine of Laguardia – well, it is not a 'Marqués de Riscal', but it is damned good, and I wish I had a barrel of it on its way to me now. It is usually sold quite young; that is, within two years of its being made. It usually goes to Bilbao, whence the brokers and wine-merchants come out and buy. It has a delicious, fresh, young virility that reminds one of that rarity, an honest Beaujolais when drunk at the *chais*. It also has much the same integrity and touch of sharpness. Whether it would travel or not I do not know, but I shall contrive to find out.

Apart from the delicious wine of Laguardia, the town itself is interesting architecturally, with two very splendid medieval and Renaissance churches like small cathedrals; the town itself is unspoilt, essentially lived in, and a small edition of Avila or Aigues Mortes, with a bursting prosperity of its own within its medieval walls and houses – and, don't forget, no motor-cars.

I lunched in Logroño, where Franco Espagnol produces 'Viña Sole', a good wine, dry and sharp. After that I visited the village of Fuenmayor in the Rioja Alta, and received a welcome at Bodegas Las Veras from Señor Cruz García Lafuente, who is eighty-three years old and the shepherd of his flock. He is called the shepherd because he started his working life as a shepherd-boy at the age of eleven. So far as I can see, he now owns a large part of the Rioja, and he certainly controls one of the three large bodegas in Fuenmayor. During this time he has fathered a flock of fourteen children; he is a firm believer in the beneficial effect of Riojan wines.

We were shown wines of the three large bodegas in the area, Bodegas Las Veras, Bodegas del Romeral, and Bodegas Entrena; and, while the wines varied slightly, they were all of a good quality and made from grapes of all the three districts of the Rioja, but mostly from the Rioja Alavesa and the Rioja Baja, these latter because of their high alcoholic content. The first fermentation takes place in cement vats, and the must is moved after ten or twelve days to similar vats for the secondary fermentation, and then put into wood for the second year and for a further two or three years, after which it is either sold, mostly in barrel, or bottled. Bodegas Las Veras is a very big concern indeed, dispatching between 100,000 and 120,000 litres every day and keeping something like 20,000,000 litres of wine in stock, maturing in the vast bodegas. Belgium and Switzerland are its chief markets, and more wine is exported than is sold domestically – which is rather a rare condition. I was given to drink two kinds of 'Reserva Especial', one white and one red, and both bearing the date 1956 on the label, which I assume to be a *reserva* date; but both wines were of excellent Rioja quality. I was also given a five-year-old 'Viña Tera', which is a comparatively cheap wine; however, I found it smooth to the palate and with a minimum of tannin. A long day finished in the Rioja, and it was dark when I said good-bye to the shepherd before returning to Logroño.

The two best-known wines of the Rioja are without doubt the

'Marqueses' made by the two bodegas one of which is owned by the Marqués de Riscal and the other by the Marqués de Murrieta. These bodegas, although quite a long way away from each other (Riscal is in the Rioja Alavesa, and Murrieta is at Ygay, a few kilometres from Logroño, roughly where the three Riojas meet), have certain methods in common that are unique in Spain. In these two bodegas, and also, incidentally, in that of López de Heredia, you find something approaching *château* bottling; but – and it is an important but – it is not quite the same.

The wines of both these great bodegas are made partly from their own grapes, but also largely from carefully selected grapes brought in and made into wine at the bodega. The grapes are carefully pressed; they are fermented in oak vats, and they receive their secondary fermentation in barrels, where they are racked three times in the first year, and so on. Now, there is a difference, for they are not necessarily bottled at the same time; and, although in the case of Riscal the cork is branded with the name of the bodega and the date, and the wine is always of that date, at Murrieta the corks are not so branded, but the date is printed on the label, and it is a true date (the year, however, as I have remarked before, is not so important). Riscal makes, for all practical purposes, only two red wines and markets them in two qualities, at six years old and older. The bodega produces a very tiny amount of white wine, rather as Château Margaux does in the Médoc. Murrieta makes three red and three white wines, but I must emphasize that the wine that is made in these two world-famous bodegas approximates most to the great wine-making *châteaux* of Bordeaux and the Côte d'Or. As to which is the better wine of the two, in the absence of any great difference in the years – well, who shall say whether Ahmed's beard or Mahmound's was the longer? No doubt they have their ideas, but I found it hard to choose.

The bodega of the Marqués de Riscal at Elciego is interesting in that it is divided by the main road; not a very big main road, admittedly, but still a road. The Marqués de Riscal claims by some ancient law to have the right of way between one side of his bodega and the other, so that the barrels can be trundled across in safety – and woe betide an

Plate 8. Valdepeñas: some majestic *tinajas* (*see* Chapter 5)

Kenneth Swain

unfortunate motorist who hits a man trundling a barrel to the hurt of
the man or the loss of the barrel. I gather that this right of way has not
yet been contested, and to make sure of the matter there is an aged
pensioner on duty who controls the proceedings. The bodegas themselves are very much like so many middle-sized French Bordeaux
châteaux, but (and I mean no bad reflection when I say this) they are
not so highly-finished. The *chais* in France is usually a spacious affair,
with polished barrels inside for fermentation; not so in the usual
Spanish bodega, including Riscal. The barrels in it hold excellent wine,
but superficially there are plenty of cobwebs – though I'm sure the
wine is not a whit the worse for this. At the back of the bodega there is a
private cellar of the wines of Marqués de Riscal, where, as in Mouton
Rothschild and Latour in Bordeaux, wines have been kept from every
vintage since, I believe, 1862. This is very impressive, and I imagine
most of them are still drinkable, for the lasting qualities of these Rioja
wines are extraordinary. I was given to taste the 'Marqués de Riscal'
1961, which was excellent, and a bottle of 1946 was decanted from the
private cellar. This was all one could expect of a twenty-year-old wine,
rich red, and having thrown an absolute minimum of crust that hardly
clouded the last inch of the bottle.

I should like to have met the Marquis of Riscal to discuss his wines,
but, although he was in, he was not receiving. Nevertheless one of his
men showed me around, and after all I came to look at the wine.

The bodega of the Marqués de Murrieta at Ygay is also rather like a
French *château*, but the atmosphere is rather different from Riscal, with
an extremely friendly welcome from the resident director, who showed
me around the *bodega de elaboración* with considerable pride. I could
form no opinion as to which of the two marquises produced the more
wine; but, of course, Murrieta makes some excellent white wines, and
most of the wine, but not quite all, is made from his own grapes. The
tinto grapes are the Tempranillo and the Mazuela, with very little
Graciano and as little as possible Garnacha; the white wine is mostly
made from the Viura grape, with a little Malvasía. Wine is not kept in
bottle here, and, although it is shipped as the wine of a certain year, it
is kept in wood until it is required. In addition to the red and white,

they make a little *rosado* too. The red wines, which I think are the chief glory of this vineyard, come in three classes: 'Marqués de Murrieta' *tinto*; 'Marqués de Murrieta Reserva Especial', which is a much older wine; and the 'Castillo Ygay', which is the *marque* for the Marqués de Murrieta's very old wine. I was given to taste the 1942 'Castillo Ygay', both *blanco* and *tinto*; they were both quite excellent, and I leave it at that merely because I have run out of superlatives. I can only suggest that you should call and taste for yourself, and I am sure you will get the same friendly reception that I did.

Obviously it was impossible for me to visit all the great bodegas of the large Rioja area, and I feel an apology is due to those whom I have been unable to report on. I have, however, tasted wines from many of these bodegas, and they are all uniformly good; some are excellent. The fairest thing to do is to give a list of all the exporters of fine wines from the Rioja, and this will be found in Appendix 2.

The famous Rioja trade-mark (*see* p. 59)

CHAPTER 5

The Wines of La Mancha and Valdepeñas

The wine-growing district of La Mancha is situated in four provinces – Toledo, Albacete, Cuenca, and Ciudad Real; Valdepeñas is in this last province. La Mancha, which is to Spanish wine-growing largely what the Midi is to France, supplies most of Spain with the sound, cheap wine sold in its wine-shops, straight from the barrel at about eight pesetas a litre, as you bring your own bottle; this corresponds roughly to sevenpence or eight cents for an average English bottle of about one and a third pints. Thus, this excellent wine is brought within the reach of all, for the benefit of mankind in general, and in particular of those people lucky enough to live in Spain.

The annual output of La Mancha is 800,000,000 litres, and 75 per cent of it or more is sold on the domestic market. The name La Mancha is derived from the Moorish *marzo*, which means 'dry land'; and this plain is very suitable for the cultivation of vines because the strong summer sun favours the ripening of the grapes. La Mancha wines, in common with other wines in Spain and especially the Rioja, gained considerably from the phylloxera scourge that all but wiped out French vineyards in the last two or three decades of the nineteenth century. To keep the trade going, the French imported vast quantities of wine from Spain, and especially from La Mancha, where the wine was suitable for blending with the native French wines, and was perfectly honest, clean wine to boot. With the end of phylloxera and the importation of immune stocks from America, this trade tended to drop; but by that time the Spanish wine-merchants of Valdepeñas had learnt a thing or two and had created and developed markets of their own. They, in turn, were treated to a dose of phylloxera, but Valdepeñas suffered least of all, and there are still pre-phylloxera vine-stocks growing there.

Good sound wine is made throughout the whole area of La Mancha, and it is made in the overall average quality of the wine, except that certain areas specialize in quantity rather than quality, and the rougher wines are distilled into alcohol and are not sold for table consumption. The best wine – although you might have some difficulty in persuading the vintners of Toledo, Albacete, and Cuenca about this – is centred in the town of Valdepeñas, which boasts 30,000 inhabitants and around 400 bodegas large, small, and medium. In Spain, Valdepeñas is synonymous with wine, and, like Jerez, the whole town is born, is married, and dies with the smell of the grape in its nostrils. Bodegas or at least a bodega can be found in every street, and through the heavy double doors, with the graceful wrought-iron lunettes over them, can be seen the cool, whitewashed courtyard and sometimes great *atrojes*, which are the cages into which the crushed grapes are poured, and in which they are pressed under their own weight before the juice starts its journey to one of the dozens of clay *tinajas*.

La Mancha is the ancient world of Don Quixote, and there is still a substantial – but alas! declining – trade in those wines that are contained in *pellejos*, or wine-skins made from a single skin of the pig and still in the same form. The wine can be kept for long periods in these skins, and the connoisseurs of the wine-shops in Madrid prefer it that way. The *pellejos* hold between 100 and 125 litres of wine. And very odd they look.

Valdepeñas produces no great or even fine wines, and does not try to compete with the Rioja, for instance, where great pride is taken in its ageing and some care in its making. Your bodega-owner in Valdepeñas is slightly contemptuous of the whole proceeding; to him wine must be well made, from sound grapes, sold quickly, and drunk fresh. Valdepeñas can be ready to drink, clear and bright, in three or four months, but this is unusual. Normally the wine is sold from its original fermenting clay *tinaja* round about the spring following the vintage. It is simply pumped out of the *tinaja*, filtered (sometimes), and then poured straight into either a *bocoy* (barrel of 800 litres) or a *barrica* (hogshead of 225 litres). Sometimes it is bottled into a *garrafa* of sixteen litres, which is a wicker-covered glass jar; it also comes in a small size of four litres only. Thus the wine travels in vast quantities to Madrid and Spain generally and in small quantities abroad. We can best examine the process from the beginning.

The vineyards of La Mancha start around the mountains of Toledo in the north of the district where they adorn the mountains; and they cover the landscape in the centre of the plains around Ciudad Real, Manzanares, and Valdepeñas, where the country is flat, with occasional low hills. The otherwise rather dull landscape is made much more attractive by these vineyards, which get larger as Valdepeñas is approached, until, in the town itself, the vineyards reach to its very walls on every side. The soil is correspondingly rich, although it varies somewhat and is of a lovely chestnut colour. It is ploughed and levelled, and each vine is planted in its own square of eighty centimetres and cultivated to a depth of forty-five centimetres, thus making a pocket of loose soil that will retain the moisture. The soil and the vines demand a good deal of rain, which is usual in this part of Spain during the winter, and the size of the grape will depend largely upon the rainfall.

A total of 1,500 vines is thus planted in a hectare, and each vine should, in an average year, produce about three kilos of sound grapes. There are four main types of grapes grown, two white and two black. The white grapes, making the *vino de mesa blanco*, are the Airen, the principal grape grown in the Valdepeñas district, and the Vidoncha, which is more prolific and produces a large quantity of wine of an indifferent quality; this is often sold for distillation into alcohol. The black grapes, which make the *tintos*, are the Cencibel, in the Valdepeñas district, and the Garnacha in other districts.

The vintage begins about the end of September, and, as I write this on the 21st of September, the first load of white grapes is just coming into the Bodegas Morenito under the keen eye of its owner, Señor Don Gerardo Sánchez. After being weighed, they are fed into the machine that removes the stalks; the crushed grapes are pumped up into the *atrojes*, which will contain, when full, 28,000 kilos of crushed grapes, and will soon be spurting the grape-juice through their slatted sides. After as much juice as possible has been squeezed out of the grapes by the colossal weight of those above them, the remainder of the husks will be put into wine-presses for a second and mechanical pressing, after which the dehydrated husks, which are dry indeed by the time they have had their second pressing, are consigned to an enormous pit; thence they are carried away for distillation into some form of alcohol. In Valdepeñas, and in Spain generally, the bodega-owner will not make his own *marc* or *eau-de-vie* as in France – and no great loss at that, for some of the liquid razor-blades distilled by the French peasant do not make the kind of liquid with which one should insult one's stomach.

The grape-juice is then pumped into the *tinaja* awaiting it. These *tinajas* stand in long, cool rows often below ground level. They are shaped like great Ali Baba jars, and they can contain anything from 3,000 to 12,000 litres. They are truly great works of potters' art, and, while they are being replaced to some extent by cement and glass-lined vats, they are still in general use and are likely to remain so, for most of the Valdepeñans consider, and I think probably rightly, that the best wine is made in the clay vessels. The *tinaja*, so much a feature of the wine of La Mancha, is built, rather than turned, by a man inside it, until it reaches shoulder height, when the top is put on and the whole 'welded' together, after which the potter climbs out of the hole in the top. Many of these splendid pots are of considerable age; some have passed their three score years and ten. When, by reason of their great strength, they achieve four score years or more, they tend to break suddenly (usually during the night, I am told), and, if they happen to be full of wine, as they sometimes are, it makes a bad day for the owner of the bodega, who is welcomed on his arrival by a place swimming with wine; he has to buy a new *tinaja*, which in these days costs something like seven or eight thousand pesetas. The wine, by the way, is scooped up off the floor with maledictions and sent to a distillery – at any rate, it isn't wasted. When the new *tinaja* arrives, it is erected in the place of the old one, and the bung-holes are then drilled out in the right position, and it is ready for immediate action.

Here the wine goes through its first boisterous fermentation, which can last as long as a month or more. It is not moved to storage-vats for its second fermentation, but is left in the *tinaja*; the sludge sinks to the bottom, and within a few weeks the wine becomes perfectly bright and clear. It is interesting to walk along the gallery at the top of these huge pots. Their mouths are covered by what appear to be conical straw hats. When one of these is removed, you can see the wine lapping the brim. It is crystal clear and very drinkable.

Valdepeñas *tinto* has none of the dark colour of most Spanish *tintos*; it is more of a *rosé* wine than red. The *tintos* are made from both white and black grapes, in the approximate proportion of 35 kilos of black grapes to 105 kilos of white. It is only in the case of *rosé*, or *rosado*, wines, which are much paler and start life in exactly the same way as the *tintos*, that the wine is siphoned off after only fifteen days of fermentation into another *tinaja*, leaving behind in the original pot the black grape-skins that give the wine its colour, before fermentation has finally dissolved the colour pigment in the skins.

The white wines vary in colour considerably, from the very pale colour of the French or German white wines to the more usual richer gold of the true Valdepeñas. The colour does not denote any change in quality; neither is the wine necessarily finer for being pale. Insofar as there is a regulator in the making of the wine, the colouring is controlled largely by the amount of grape-skins that are left in the wine for fermentation.

Beyond this, nothing much happens; and, as we have seen, the vinification process is simple indeed. As one bodega-owner said to me, 'We are famous here for not knowing anything about oenology – the wine makes itself'. The whole process can be summed up as follows. The grape-juice is put into the *tinajas*, where it receives its first and secondary fermentations, and it is drawn off through a bung-hole about eighteen inches from the bottom of the *tinaja*, leaving the sludge under the bung-hole; the less pure elements are removed from an even lower bung-hole and sent away for distillation into alcohol. Thereafter a man will descend into this vast pot and clean it out ready for the next vintage.

One of the more important virtues of this excellent wine is its lasting property, which is remarkable when you consider how young the wines are at the time of sale. I travelled in Spain extensively in 1950, and it was then that I enjoyed my first Spanish wine; I brought home with me a bottle of Valdepeñas wine, among a few other kinds, and put it in my cellar with various white wines to see if the Valdepeñas did, in fact, travel well. The other wines were all consumed over the years, and they were all good; but the Valdepeñas was overlooked, and I discovered it only two months ago (that is, in the summer of 1965), when it had been in my cellar for no fewer than fifteen years. I produced it at lunch with a Spanish wine-shipper, and it was excellent and had not only kept perfectly but had even improved. Valdepeñas wines have a faint earthy tang, which I personally rather enjoy, but this had gone from the fifteen-year-old wine, and its excellence had all the dignity of age.

Generally speaking, most of the bodegas keep a few old wines that they refresh under a simple kind of solera system, similar to that used with Sherry, but they attach no importance to it and keep the wines merely as interesting exhibits or for their own consumption, and they are not for sale. At the Bodegas Morenito I was given a solera wine of this type, which started as a straight white Valdepeñas forty years ago, but is now golden brown and has developed strong Madeira characteristics; certainly it is nothing like an ordinary Valdepeñas. The white wine from a 1901 solera that I was given at the Bodegas Bilbainas was a very strong wine indeed and not altogether to my taste. It had a very pleasant 'woody' characteristic, however, and indeed tasted like old Sherry. I believe that this is sold in small quantities as an *elaboración especial*. Apparently you have to ask for it to get it, although the solera is quite large.

Bodegas Bilbainas also make other types of wine from varieties of natural Valdepeñas. This is unusual, though, and very few bodegas indulge in this kind of vinous exercise, which is not always successful. Among the types of wine that I saw in this large bodega was a *mistela*, which is luscious and sweet, rather like a muscatel with its grape flavour; it is made by the addition of a small quantity of brandy to stop

Plate 9. La Mancha, land of *pellejos* and *tinajas*: a scene
at Bodegas Morenito, Valdepeñas

George Rainbird

fermentation after fifteen days, before the sugar has been completely broken down. At this bodega they also make altar wine, which is pale and has to be filtered and be of absolute purity in order to satisfy the exacting requirements of the Church authorities. Another by-product is a rather special Vermouth, which is not unpleasant and has considerable character, of the Italian rather than the French type. These wines can be and often are made at any bodega; but, as I have said before, most of the Valdepeñans stick to making their extremely simple but good wines without bothering about refinements or developments of them.

The wine of La Mancha is made in a completely natural way, and, although there are no official regulations forbidding *chaptalisation*, no sugar is added to assist the wine. The natural wine of Valdepeñas and La Mancha generally has a vinosity of 13° to 13½° of alcohol in the white wines, and 13½° to 14° in the *tintos*: this, of course, constitutes quite a heady wine and is much stronger than the *ordinaires* of the Midi, which vary between 9° and 11°. It is the *vino típico* of Madrid, and, even at the best restaurants, if you order a jug of wine with your dinner, say at Botin, you are almost certain to get the best Valdepeñas. And very good it is.

When in Valdepeñas I had the pleasure of visiting two of the larger bodegas and one of the very smallest.

The two larger were Bodegas Morenito owned by Señor Don Gerardo Sánchez, and Bodegas Bilbainas of Señor Don Joaquín Ugarte. In point of fact, Morenito owned two large bodegas with over 400 *tinajas* – indeed an impressive sight. Bilbainas again have a large bodega here, with the air of having been at one time even larger, although it is prosperous today. The distillery there has a tall factory-like chimney with a stork's nest on the top. Upon inquiring what they did about the storks when they lit the fire, I was informed that, since it meant disturbing the storks, they had decided to give up distillation in Valdepeñas, and they no longer made any brandy or liqueurs there. But I don't think they ever made much brandy, and they must have decided in any case to give it up.

The small bodega owned by Señor Don Hilario de la Torre was

remarkable. Señor de la Torre is a small farmer, and in one courtyard, which I paced out at forty feet square (leading off it is his bodega with its *tinajas*), he has his wine-press, and, at the time that I was there, ten excellent cows, one of which yielded thirty litres of milk a day, and a day-old calf. It was all rather crowded, but the glass of last year's wine I was shown was certainly equal to any Valdepeñas I had drunk. Señor de la Torre has his own vineyard, and he grows enough grapes to make 48,000 litres of this excellent *vino blanco*. There are dozens of other bodegas of this size, and hundreds bigger, all over this quiet town with heavily grilled windows. But the quietude departs for a few days at the time of the vintage, when the tumbrils and *camiones* laden with grapes rumble through the streets on the way to their owner's or some other factor's bodega to be made into wine.

After Valdepeñas, a great deal of these good wines are made at El Tomelloso, which is a town of 30,000 people living almost exclusively from wine and its derivatives, including a brandy for which they are particularly noted. Manzanares (which is only twenty-six kilometres from Valdepeñas), Alcazar de San Juan, Cinco Casas, and Daimiel are also noted wine-producing centres. The wine is sometimes marketed under a particular vineyard label, but it is never dated as that of a given year, because there isn't all that much difference between one year and another. There are, of course, a few wines sold with a vine-yard label, and some even with the date; but your bodega-owner of Valdepeñas laughs at this kind of thing, and, as one told me, 'If you see a bottle of Valdepeñas with the date on it, you need not necessarily believe it – nobody in Valdepeñas would'.

CHAPTER 6

The Wines of Málaga

Málaga used to be much drunk in England in the days when rich, fruity wines were in favour. It was also sometimes called 'Mountain', because the grapes are grown and some of the wine itself is made in the mountainous country behind Málaga. It is a very large area indeed, ranging as far as Antequera in the north, but most of the vineyards are to be found in the neighbourhood of the Sierra de Almijara.

The wines are without exception sweet, and, while the driest type called *seco* is not quite so sticky as tawny port, it is still on the sweet side, although very agreeable.

There is a considerable recorded history of Málaga grapes that goes back to Roman republican days; Columella, writing in 44 B.C., deals with them very fully and classifies them by cultivation, quality, and even soil and specifies whether they were used for eating or for the making of wine. Most of the grapes in the Málaga district are in fact table grapes. Democritus, Pliny, and Virgil in his *Georgics*, mention the excellence and diversity of the wine. There are also many records from Moorish sources, which is rather surprising in view of the fact that the drinking of wine was prohibited by Mohammed; the Koran has some extremely nasty things to say about wine-drinking in general, but even in those days of prohibition the Moors sometimes managed to dodge the arm of the law, to the benefit of their bodies if not of their souls. One writer refers to an old Muslim who, in his last hours, was exhorted by the Imam to ask the forgiveness of Allah for his many sins, among which was his liking for wine; the dying man prayed, 'O Creator of all things, I implore you not to leave me in Paradise without Málaga wine'.

The Spanish chroniclers, after the liberation from the Moors, refer constantly to this wine, and Ruiz González de Clavijo, who visited the city of Málaga in May 1403, speaks of the Sierra de Málaga in very glowing terms; not the least of its attractions was the sight of mountains covered with vines and orchards. In the eighteenth century the Andalusian ambassador to Catherine the Great of Russia presented her with forty-eight cases of assorted Málaga wines, and that famous, or infamous, empress replied with a very enthusiastic letter saying that she was very fond of these wines of Spain, as she called them. In 1792 a priest, who thought it better to write under the *nom de plume* of Cecilio García de la Lena, wrote a book dedicated to the 'Very Illustrious and Ancient Brotherhood of Málaga Vineyard Owners', and this included a complete list of the varieties of grapes grown and the wines made at that time; among the grapes were mentioned the famous Pedro Ximénez, Jaén Blanco, Almunecar, Moscatelon or Moscatel Flamenco (which Pliny called Apianas, because bees liked the fruit), Don Bueno, Cabriel, Casiles Albillas, and Teta de Vaca. Of course the famous P.X. is still the favourite grape, and, together with Moscatel, Jaén Blanco, Jaén Doradillo, and Rome, it is still extensively used.

True Málaga is made from a mixture of these grapes and is rather more than half P.X., only 15 per cent Moscatel, about 20 per cent Lairén (which cuts the sweetness a little), and about 5 per cent of other grapes.

Most of the wine of Málaga is made in the villages, but an ever-increasing proportion is made from must that is collected from the presses and brought into Málaga in tankers and transferred into the enormous oak fermenting-vats, where it is kept for about a year before being filtered into oak butts; most of it is sold after a further period of one to three years, or blended for the old soleras that still exist.

In the villages, which are not seen easily from the coast road but lie off in the mountains to the west of the city, the presses are busy from about the end of August onwards; largely because of the mountainous

Plate 10. The vintage near Valdepeñas
(*see* Chapter 5)

George Rainbird

terrain, the vineyards are invariably small, few being of more than ten acres. My friend Harry Yoxall, to whom I am indebted for a great deal of information on Málaga wines, says in his excellent article in the *Wine and Food Journal* (1965, Autumn number) that there are something like 22,000 acres of vines in the *denominación de origen* area of Málaga, but much of this area is for the cultivation of table grapes rather than for wine.

Under the guidance of Señor Ankersmit I visited the large bodega of Scholtz Hermanos, where the tankers of must had been received from the mountain vineyards and pumped into the enormous oak fermentation-vats, some of which hold as much as 20,000 gallons each, and of which there were perhaps a dozen or more. Over the years, the types of Málaga have become more or less standardized, and most of the big bodegas produce wine of corresponding quality, although some of them have one or two very old soleras, of which they are justly proud. The wine from these soleras is not sold, but is used for blending with the much younger wines to give them true character, which it certainly does. Yoxall mentions having been privileged to taste a 'Lágrima 1787', which runs to 17·4° of alcohol. I was myself given a 'Solera Scholtz 1874', which is really a delicious wine and quite free from the overpowering sweetness of an old P.X. solera. I cannot do better than to quote Yoxall where he describes the wine of these ancient soleras: 'There are interesting, almost surprising undertones beneath its unctuous richness, like the dark fires in the heart of a jewel'.

Málaga 'Lágrima' (*lágrima* in Spanish means a tear) is not to be confused with the Lacrima Cristi of Italy, which is a different wine altogether.

The different types of wine made in Málaga and sold as Málaga are as follows:

Negro	Made mostly from P.X. grapes, and very dark indeed.
Blanco dulce	Golden brown to dark amber, and very sweet.
Semidulce	Rather lighter in colour, not quite so sweet, but sweet nevertheless.
Oscuro	A rich chestnut colour.
Amontillado	Made from Lairén grapes, medium dry, and usually sold before its tenth year.
'Lágrima'	Very sweet and dark.

F

Seco   Rather similar, as I have said, to tawny port but slightly drier and better to my taste; as an aperitif wine with a dry biscuit at eleven o'clock in the morning, it would equal what bank managers of yore are supposed to have offered their clients.

There are many other variations on the same theme, but in general these are dessert wines of excellence and, to my taste, preferable to the sweet muscatels of France and Italy.

A certain amount of brandy, *anís*, gin, and *ponche* (still in its silver bottle) is made in the Málaga district, and I was a little depressed to hear from Señor Ankersmit that the sale of spirits was expanding although the sale of wine has tended to decline. To this, the tremendous development of the Costa del Sol, with its rash of tourist hotels and fantastic influx of international, spirit-drinking visitors from abroad, may have made some contribution. Be that as it may, I hope to see the situation reversed before I die. Casual visitors to Málaga, should they have time to visit a bodega, might do worse than to visit Garrijo, in the centre of the town; it has a deservedly busy long bar, in which every kind of Málaga wine and spirits is served straight from the wood at about two pesetas a glass.

The wines of Málaga are quite pure and without added alcohol; for this reason, apart from their other qualities, they have long been popular with the Church authorities as sacramental wines, which must be pure in every respect. This important trade is in the hands of two bodegas that work closely with the Church authorities. I have had my own experience of this, for, several years ago, I bought at an auction a lot of old wines among which were 'eight bottles believed to be altar wine'. None of the wine in the lot was later than 1900 (it included, I remember, some 1870 Château Margaux), and these eight bottles were indeed older; one of them still had a nineteenth-century label stating 'Finest altar wine guaranteed pure by the Most Reverend the Lord Bishop of Málaga' – which is exactly what it was, very old Málaga that, because of its great age, was no longer over-sweet and was absolutely delicious. I fear, however, that it did not reach the altar.

Having examined the bodega system in Málaga and drunk of the wines thereof, I decided to go up into the Sierra de Almijara and taste the wines in the area where most of the grapes are grown and where some of the wine is made. The road runs through El Palo, Cala del Moral, and Torre del Mar, all of which towns are suffering from the *urbanización* that is making such an unhappy mark on the Costa del Sol. Turning off the main coastal road at La Caleta for ten or twelve kilometres up into the mountains, the road runs at first through fields of sugar-cane, beans, and similar market-garden crops, but soon the tarred surface gives up, and you are left with a comparatively narrow unsurfaced road, tying itself into knots around and through the foothills of the mountains. Vines now start to be grown abundantly; and everywhere, as far as the eye can reach, the tiny, immaculate white cottages of the small farmers can be seen going right to the top of the lower mountains. As the vineyards climb higher, the terraces get smaller, so that near the top they seem only two or three feet wide, yet all are perfectly cultivated; they reminded me a great deal of the Inca terrace system of cultivation in the High Andes, though, since the Incas terraced their hills long before the Spanish came, one supposes that this system of utilizing cultivable land is as old as civilization. I passed the village of Algarrobo, white in the sun, with tropical flowers growing abundantly up the sides of the houses, and in six kilometres of hair-raising driving came to the village of Sayalonga and drove into the main square, which was all of fifty feet from one side to the other, where the car was soon surrounded by interested and curious inhabitants.

Inquiries were then made as to whether there was a wine-press in the village, and I was courteously escorted to the village wine-shop and presented to Señor Don Rafael Alcoba, who is the owner of the best and largest vineyards in the village, amounting to some twenty hectares. I told him that I should like, if possible, to look at his bodega and see how he made his wine and to taste it. He expressed himself as being delighted to show me his bodega, and, while we were talking, I was given a glass of excellent 'Mountain', medium gold in colour, dryer than I had tasted in Málaga, and delicious. I was assured that this had been made in the village, and the proprietor of the wine-shop said he was very much pleased to be able to demonstrate his excellent wine; he refused all payment. Don Rafael then led the way through this charming village with its up-and-down streets, fortunately unnavigable by motor-cars, the houses freshly painted and with flowers all over them and hanging across the streets everywhere.

The bodega proved to be, as I expected, quite a small one, making 300 *arrobas* (one *arroba* equals about sixteen litres) of 'Mountain' in a good year. The grapes are gathered and include a preponderance of P.X.; so far as I could see, however, no effort was made to mix the grapes in any kind of proportion. Mixed they certainly were, but I would hardly call the mixture scientific. Yet the result seemed none the worse for it. The grapes are carried in on muleback and discharged into a treading-bin, where the wine is trampled out of them by foot; I was delighted and surprised to hear this. When there is nothing left but the skins, pips, stalks, and so forth, these go into a rather primitive press, with a layer of the residue covered first by a grass mat; then by another layer of residue; then by another mat; and then by a few more inches of residue. When the press is full, this gigantic sandwich of mat and residue is pressed and the remaining drops of juice are collected. The juice from the treading and the press flows into a sump, and from there it is taken out in buckets and poured into 300-litre oak *botas*, where it has its first fermentation, taking about fifteen days, and then its secondary fermentation, after which it is racked into fresh *botas*. There it is kept for a year; then it is sold, or kept for another year and sold at a higher price. Don Rafael sells his wine to the wine-shops in Málaga, and I think most of the better wines made in the villages probably go the same way; but the bulk of the wine goes to the bodegas in Málaga, as we have seen. I was given to taste of the last year's vintage, and I found it, of its kind, excellent. Later I was privileged to try, at the owner's house, a glass of his older wine, which was even better, still rather sweet to my taste, but undoubtedly excellent 'Mountain'.

Continuing my tour, I passed through a small farmyard that adjoined Don Rafael's bodega; there half-a-dozen attractive young women were sorting and packing fat raisins. From the stacks of almond shells, I judged that that harvest had already been gathered in and was probably on its way to England. I was then escorted to the house of a neighbour, who owned a few vines and who made possibly one *bota* of wine, part of which he no doubt sold while he kept another part for his own consumption; and there he was, happy as a sandboy, with the must streaming freely from his *alpargatas de esparto*, treading his own grapes on his tiny treading-floor. Outside, on a sunny bank, the grapes were spread to dry in the sun; they alternated in rows, as those that would become raisins and those that were to be brought to the right degree of sweetness for wine. I counted at least five different sorts of grapes in the collection, both black and white; one was a large golden grape called Ojos del Rey (literally translated, this means 'eyes of the king'), which I for one had certainly never heard of before.

This is one of the springs that eventually make up the mighty river of Málaga wine flowing into that city; and the same operation must be going on at this time of writing all over that very wide area. I turned back to continue my travels, leaving Don Rafael with some considerable regret. He was a grave, courteous man who was having difficulty in finding help and was reducing the area of his vines, the trouble being, of course, the attraction to the bright lights and the prosperity that is being created by the tourist trade. Sayalonga was a town of about fourteen hundred souls, and, if twenty hectares is by far the largest holding, the average must be small indeed.

CHAPTER 7

The Wines of the Levante

A great deal – in fact, an enormous quantity – of wine is made along the Levantine coast and for some great distance inland, being exported and distributed through the Levantine ports of Alicante, Almería, and Valencia. Nearly all these wines are simply made, honest wines, produced without any attempt at finesse, and they cater for quick and cheap consumption by those who like their wine heavy and, by comparison, sweet. Within this general classification, however, there are degrees, and now and again one comes across some excellent wine that is worthy of comparison with some of the finer wines made in Spain. Levante wines are mostly red, but a good deal of ordinary white wine is made in the Alicante district and is sometimes blended into better quality wines. The alcoholic content ranges from 13° to 16°, and higher if the wine is allowed to age. They are all good table wines, if somewhat coarse by certain standards, but with none of the roughness that is associated with common wines from other Mediterranean countries. A good example is Benicarló, a dark, rich red wine from Castellón de la Plana.

The wines of Murcia are mostly produced in a long valley, where the two wine-making centres are the towns of Jumilla and Yecla, in which most of the bodegas are situated. However, the vines are grown for a long way on both sides of these towns. They are right at the north of the province of Murcia, and, in fact, the vine-belt continues a considerable way into the province of Valencia; but the wines there, although similar, are slightly different in character and somewhat drier. The road to Jumilla from Murcia is rather devious and constitutes a most delightful drive, even if it is hard on the springs, at 800 metres (about 2,500 feet) above sea-level. The wines made here are all *tintos*, from the Morastrell grape, which has some affinity with the Pinot *noir* of France, in that the grapes are small and are formed in tightly packed bunches, clustered around the main trunk of the vine. Wine-grapes, and indeed all fruits, are grown in profusion in this valley, and a great many table grapes are grown here too, but they are grown on a somewhat different system, the vine being formed into a long trunk rather like that of a standard rose in England; the leaves are suspended on a wire framework so that the grapes hang down from underneath. The wine-grapes are grown in the conventional Spanish style, with roughly 1,500 vines to the hectare, and are pruned to five or six shoots.

The grapes are not made into wine by the growers but are sold to bodegas in Jumilla or Yecla. On the way to Jumilla I stopped at an *estancia* belonging to Señor Don Jesús García, and was informed that the vintage had begun and he was busy at his bodega in Jumilla. To this I duly presented myself; I was courteously shown over it by Señor García's son, and was given some of these good Jumilla wines to taste. As in Valdepeñas, the grapes, having been cleared of their stalks, are smashed and pumped into very big cement primary-fermentation-vats after which time the must is pumped into underground vats to complete its tumultuous fermentation, which takes a further seven or eight days. When the first fermentation is complete, the resulting wine is pumped into a large number of storage-vats in an adjoining bodega, where it remains for three months, after which it is filtered and is ready for selling, although usually the wines are not sold for some seasons after that. I was given a Murcian wine from the 1964 vintage; it contained about 16° alcohol. I found it good, but obviously strong and rather sweet; a little cloying to the taste, in fact. It appeared to have little tannin in it. These were obviously honest, well made wines, but, as might be expected, they lacked any kind of delicacy. I was also given a wine that was seven years old; it had 18° alcohol and was somewhat drier with age, having lost none of its essential character.

Most of the Murcian wines are of this sort, but in Alicante a great quantity of rich, sweet wine is made from the Moscatel, Malvasía, and Garnacha grapes, mostly the first; and it has the usual character of muscatel wines in that it tastes of the grape and it has a very high alcohol content. There is a further type of wine grown in Alicante called 'Fondillon', which is normally not sold until it is ten years old; it is limited in quantity and fetches a higher price than the other wines of the region. The best Alicante wines are grown in the valley of Vina-lope, which produces excellent table wines, mostly *rosados* but including a few *tintos* and *blancos*. The *rosados* and *tintos* contain 13° to 16° of alcohol.

In Valencia, where the coastal plain is extremely fruitful and rich, a much larger variety of vines is cultivated. As well as the Morastrell, which I have already described, the Morenilla, Malvasía, Moscatel, Bobal, Garnacha, and our old friend Pedro Ximénez produce between them a great number of wines, but they are all of the same basic character and include red, white, and *rosado* wines. The vintage varies somewhat according to the grape grown; it can start as early as late July and can go on until early November. In Requena, one of the towns in this province, are made wines containing as little as 9° of alcohol, whereas some of the wines produced in the region of Liria contain up to 18°. The *tintos* vary in colour from those that are little darker than *rosados* to a wine called 'Carlón', which is almost black and, though a high-grade wine, is very thick and is largely used for blending with lighter wines to give them body.

Valencia wines also include sweet, dessert wines made from the Moscatel and Pedro Ximénez grapes, and here again they reach a very high degree of alcohol – as high as 23° in certain cases. Valencia exports more wine than any other province in Spain. Most of it goes to Switzerland and Germany; I do not know what happens to it when it gets there, but the figures speak for themselves. The importance of the export market of Valencia wines can be judged by the fact that in 1964 a total quantity of 864,546 hectolitres was exported, mostly in bulk to Germany, Switzerland, Belgium, and Denmark; a certain amount of bottled wine went to the United States.

CHAPTER 8

The Wines of Catalonia

In the province of Tarragona two kinds of wine are made. One is a sweetish, heavy wine called simply Tarragona; a special variety of this is known as the Priorato. The other consists of a group of excellent clean table wines made throughout the very large Tarragona district. Priorato is a *denominación de origen* in its own right; its district, a small island within the *denominación de origen* area of Tarragona, comprises a series of small foothills to the mountains of volcanic origin, in contrast with the much larger area and better soil of the Tarragona district proper.

Tarragona has had in England what we should call, in today's parlance, a bad press or a bad public image, due to the fact that, for some decades at the end of the last century and up to the time of the First World War, Tarragona wine was imported in vast quantities and sold in public houses, largely for consumption by the ladies, at a penny or two a glass, on the general principle of 'drunk for a penny and dead drunk for twopence'. It was known as the poor man's Port or, more colloquially, as Red Biddy, and it was a ferocious liquid, made from concentrated must and with an alcoholic content of 25° or 30°. Fortunately the taxes imposed on wines with a high alcoholic content successfully put paid to Red Biddy, which had little to commend it either as a wine or a habit, but the present result is that Tarragona wine has an undeservedly bad reputation, and this prejudices the general sale of Tarragona wine in Great Britain, except to the connoisseurs who know that the modern Tarragona has nothing in common with its infamous predecessor. Just how this prejudice can be overcome I do not know, for, although the present generation has probably never heard of its ill reputation, the memory of those in the wine trade is long – and, after all, they are the people who buy the wine in the first place. If anything can be said for public relations, this might well be a job that it could and ought to tackle. The result of it all has been that Tarragona bodegas have more and more been compelled, for the export of their wines, to try to match the popular French types, which they do, but only up to a point. The trouble is that, in matching somebody else's wine, the tendency is to lose the essential character of one's own, and this I find to be happening particularly in Tarragona. The pure Tarragona wines have tremendous character, and, although Priorato is a special district within Tarragona, I propose to start with these wines as having a quite fantastic character that is unique in Spanish viniculture.

The name Priorato comes from the priory of an old Carthusian monastery, now in ruins, that already existed in the fifteenth century, called Scala Dei, situated on the slopes of the Sierra de Montsant ('Holy Mountain'); a good number of villages nearby depended on the priory. Lava in the soil here produces wines of very high alcoholic content, as it generally does elsewhere – for instance, on the slopes of Mount Etna in Sicily. Priorato has an extremely pleasant and, indeed, beautiful terrain; as usual, the vines of the Garnacha variety that are grown here produce fruit containing a very high proportion of sugar; it is also of superb quality. The vines are not particularly prolific, with two or three kilos of grapes per vine, as against some of the vineyards on the coastal plain, where, I am told, some of the vines produce as much as eight to ten kilos, and make correspondingly ordinary wine. Priorato, is, however, quite different, and the vines there make two varieties of wine. The first is a dry wine, which is completely natural when the fermentation has been allowed to take its full course. It is as black as your hat, and of such extreme dryness that it cannot be drunk with any pleasure, but it has an alcoholic content of up to 18° after fermentation; it is the perfect vehicle for giving body in the blending of other wines, and it is used almost exclusively for this purpose. With the sweet wines of Priorato, fermentation is cut at a fairly early stage by the addition of alcohol, which produces superb dessert wines with an alcoholic content of between 14° and 22°, and so 'thick' that the wine sticks to the glass. I must say that they taste a lot better than I have made them sound, as I find upon re-reading what I have just written.

In addition to these two, the dry and sweet wines, Priorato also produces large quantities of *mistela* (must in which the fermentation never starts, because it is stopped at birth); the resulting grape-juice, rightly so-called, is clarified, stored, and sold for blending and for cutting down the alcoholic strength of some of the stronger wines elsewhere in Spain and abroad, and to give them some character, which it most certainly does.

Until quite recently, the ageing of the wines was sometimes accelerated by bottling into *bombonas*, which are glass bottles holding about thirty litres and shaped rather like so many pears. This sounds extraordinary and looks extraordinary, but so they are. They were laid out in fields for about a couple of years, exposed to Mediterranean heat in summer and to the mild winter rains. It is necessarily an expensive way of doing things, and it is by now largely discontinued in this region, but I shall describe this method more when we come to the wines of Panadés, where it is still used. So much for the unique wine of Priorato, with its little vineyards and their great big wines.

Vines are grown all over the region of Tarragona; they start somewhere south in the mountainous district of Gandesa and reach to the Panadés region in the north. The wines are made in the village co-operatives, and are brought to the twin towns of Reus and Tarragona (which are of about equal size, having each perhaps 50,000 inhabitants), where lie the bodegas, large and small, in which the wines are stored and blended. I have visited two of these village cooperatives, in Valls and Santas Creus; each makes about 2,500,000 litres of wine in an average year. In the old days, the vineyard-owners made their own wine; but this no longer happens, and, though there might be an occasional small farmer who will gather his grapes and tread his wine, such a practice is now rare.

At the time of the vintage, in motoring between the villages of these lovely hills below the Sierra de Montsant, you see the farmers' carts being loaded with *portadores*, which are oval, open barrels into which the basketsful of grapes from the pickers are tipped and crushed down until they are overflowing; and all along the road stretch vehicles of every size, from the small man's mule, with perhaps two or three *portadores*, to a tractor-drawn wagon full to the brim with grapes from the larger vineyards. They are on their way to their cooperative, and as you leave the villages you mix with further streams of laden vehicles coming in and of empty ones going out. Half way between villages you begin to pass a similar stream going into the next cooperative. When such a stream arrives at the cooperative *bodega de elaboración*, each whole vehicle, including the mule or tractor, is weighed and a tally-check is given to the driver, together with a little wooden ball that has a number engraved on it. The vehicle is then taken across the yard to the receiving-bin, where the little ball is handed over with the grapes, which are discharged into the crushing-machine; at the same time the ball is put into a pipe, and it arrives simultaneously with a sample of the crushed juice in a miniature laboratory situated just under the crushing-machine. There assistants with sucrometers test the juice for sugar content, matching the number on the little ball, and the tally-check is then made out for the weight of the grapes, plus the actual Baumé content, and the owner will be paid at a fixed rate for his grapes, plus or minus so much according to their sugar content. All very simple and ingenious – and, I think, efficient. I found the whole process more than interesting.

These cooperative presses are enormous. In the Santas Creus co-operative, the whole process is scientifically and carefully organized on two levels, in an enormous Piranese-like building, with animated figures at the top shovelling in the grapes, and the monster mechanical presses squeezing out the juice at the rate of hundreds of gallons per hour (which seemed to me more like hundreds of gallons per minute), while at the other end of the press the residue of skins, pips, stalks, and what have you is discharged like a continuous sausage of greeny-brown vegetation, which again is ejected into carefully-arranged mechanical presses for a second pressing, and trampled down by bare-footed young men, with a further but smaller resulting stream of juice joining the main torrent running into the fermenting-vats from the lower level. In the case of Santas Creus, the cooperative has a smaller press mainly for a better-quality red wine (most of the wine made in this district is white), but there the stalks are removed before pressing and sacked up and sent to a distillery. This is also what happens to the *orujo*, which is the residue of the pips, stalks, and husks from the larger presses of the cooperative. In Spain there seems to be no attempt to make *marc* or *eau-de-vie* as in France. The grape-juice is pumped into underground fermenting-vats (which contain many thousands of litres of must); they are arranged in rows, and you can walk between them. The apertures are the size of manholes, and they are filled to the brim. The wine can be seen bubbling away in its first tumultuous fermentation; the floor of the bodega feels quite hot as you walk on it, and the atmosphere is heavy with the rich smell of fermenting must that pervades the whole building.

The wine goes through both stages of fermentation in these vats, and in the following spring it is usually sold to the owners of the bodegas in Tarragona or Reus, when there is a steady stream of brokers who bring in samples of the wine to the bodegas and arrange the contracts with the blenders. The minimum price, fixed by the Spanish Government, is based on a given figure per degree of alcohol per hectolitre; if trade is bad, the cooperative remains assured of a market, for the Government will purchase the wine at that figure. In practice, however, this rarely happens, as the wine is of good quality, and I am told that there is never any difficulty about selling it a peseta or two above the minimum price. The bodega-owner in Tarragona or Reus must pay for half of the wine when he contracts to buy it, and for the remainder at given periods, but he must clear the wine from the cooperative in time to leave it ready for the next vintage.

I was able to visit three bodegas in Tarragona and Reus, of varying sizes. One belongs to Señor José Antonio López Bertrán, who claims that it is the most modern in Tarragona, as it may well be, for it gleams with stainless steel and produces an enormous quantity of wine of an equally gleaming sort, clean and bright and altogether suitable for his expanding export market all over the world.

Another bodega, in Reus and belonging to the well-named Amigó brothers, is rather more old-fashioned; the storage and blending are carried out in huge oak vats in a cobwebby bodega. Señor Don Juan Amigó, who is an anglophile and extremely fluent in English, explained that, so far as he could see, the cobwebs did not affect the wine and the spiders helped to keep down the mosquitos. He makes quite excellent wine, and you can take your choice between stainless steel and cobwebs. I think there is something to be said for the latter.

The third bodega I visited was in Tarragona; it belonged to the President of the local Sindicato de la Vid, Señor Don Manuel Tapias. He produces a smaller quantity of excellent wine, and I gathered that he is not terribly anxious to make more. His well-ordered bodega produces comparatively few wines, of the true Tarragona character, which are all of excellent quality. Most of the bodegas produce true Tarragona wine, which may be dry or sweet, but is largely sweet and is extremely palatable. Moreover it is altogether honest and unfortified, and it has nothing to do with the ill-reputed Tarragonas of long ago, which were made from must that had been heated almost to boiling point, and produced the vicious liquid I have already discussed. The vinosity, even so, is quite high, rising to over 20° in the case of an old wine that may have been blended from a very much older solera. They are all delicious, and I wish they were more popular in England; perhaps they will be one day. Certainly they deserve to be.

For the rest, most of the bodegas make a straightforward dry white wine, which has a characteristic edge to it but is without acidity; it has some affinity with a clean Chablis and yet it is not a Chablis. The *semisecos* are softer and refreshing, while the sweet wines, which contain an element of Moscatel grapes, do not cloy. The white wines all contain 12° to 14° of alcohol; but the red wines, which are mostly dry, are from 14° to 16°, and again they have something of the distinctive flavour I associate with the Priorato wine that is used in the blending of most of them.

The *vino corriente* – the natural white wine, which is produced in great quantities and sold in the wine-shops and bars and forms the common wine in a restaurant – is exceedingly pleasant. It is, in fact, pale golden. The red wine is very red, verging on black. The white wines for export tend to be made very pale, because that seems to be the way the export markets want them. An excellent *rosado* is also made in Tarragona.

It is with some regret that I leave Tarragona, with its Iberian, Roman, and medieval walls, its cathedral and its ancient town. I like the wines and I like the people, and I should like, most of all, to see Tarragona wine brought back into a degree of popularity under its own excellent name.

And now for Panadés. The wines made in the district covered by this *denominación de origen* are centred on the town of Villafranca del Panadés, which is roughly half way between Tarragona and Barcelona, and the town takes a Catalonian pride in the wine it produces. The first thing you see on entering Villafranca on the road from Tarragona is the enormous wine-press at the very beginning of the town, which is a much better beginning than the usual statue to a local dignitary or a war memorial. It is an even bigger press than the ones in the Clos de Vougeot in Burgundy, as I remember them. It was in use in Panadés from the sixteenth century up to the end of the nineteenth century, and another one nearly as big is on show in the town's Museum of Viniculture. The official wine-growing district of Panadés stretches from Vendrell, about twenty kilometres from Tarragona in the south-west, to well beyond Sitges in the north-east, and terminating about twenty-four kilometres from Barcelona. Villafranca del Panadés is the principal wine-making town, and San Sadurní de Noya has also a great number of bodegas – this is where most of the Spanish sparkling wines are made.

The terrain is mainly hilly from the sea inland, reaching a height of nearly 2,000 feet in the highest parts, where as usual some of the best wines are grown. The temperature-changes throughout the area are not great, even between the sea and the mountains, and the rainfall over a long period is considered to be about perfect for vines.

Several sorts of wine are made here, and the *denominación de origen* authorities have classified the standard wines according to their degree of alcohol, from the light white Panadés, which can be as low as 9° (but which may be considerably stronger), to the red Panadés, which can be as high as 16°. The *corriente* wines are made in the upper and central

Panadés region; they are white wines of a light greenish-golden colour, and they are all well balanced, mild wines and extremely pleasant to drink.

In Villafranca del Panadés the wine museum, under the directorship of Señor Don Pablo Boada, who was kind enough to show me round, is most impressive; it gives the whole history of viniculture throughout Spain from early times. Here can and should be seen many types of Greek and Roman amphoras, with excellent and accurate models of how wine was made in different ages, and also of types of bodegas generally throughout Spain. Every kind of container is shown here, from the sublimely simple wine-cup to the ridiculous and elaborate glass bottles much in vogue at the end of the last century, often in the form of a figure of a man or woman with the neck of the bottle sticking out at the top of the head; in one silly case, a hand holds a pistol and the wine comes out of the muzzle. There are also great wine-barrels of considerable antiquity, which were in use until recently, and wine-presses of every size, shape, and age, together with a considerable gallery of wine illustrations, cartoons, posters, and so on. Here too there is, very wisely, a little bar where the typical wine of Panadés may be drunk and where pleasant and sensible little souvenirs may be purchased, such as Catalan *porrones* in various sizes or, if you cannot manage a *porrón* (and I cannot, although I have often tried), a glass to drink out of in a more Christian manner. The *porrón* is a pear-shaped flask with a spout and handle; to use it requires some skill, and I am always fascinated at seeing a virtuoso perform, sometimes holding the *porrón* at arm's length and not spilling a drop. But to return to the good wines of Panadés.

My escort on this occasion was the President of the Panadés Sindicato de la Vid, Señor Don Miguel Torres, whose dynamic energy has greatly expanded his bodega, founded by his grandfather in 1870. The wine, as in Tarragona, is usually made in the cooperatives throughout the area, and is bought by Señor Torres and his colleagues and associates in exactly the same way as in Tarragona. But, in the case of the Torres bodega, they make a certain amount of their own wine from their own vineyards, or from selected grapes that are bought from

Plate 11. The wines of Villafranca del Panadés: exposed for maturing in *bombonas* at Bodegas Torres

George Rainbird

the farmers. In Panadés the system has always been to ferment the must in barrels rather than vats, although again this is tending to die out, especially in the larger bodegas; but I am sentimental enough to regret the passing of the fermenting-cask for the tile-lined or stainless steel or cement vat. Nevertheless, even in the most scientific bodegas, the new hogsheads, pipes, *botas*, and *bocoyes* are often filled with sea-water for fourteen days to cut out the 'woody' taste that the new cask might impart to the wine; this practice is certainly followed where the wine is made near the coast, as in Tarragona, for example.

There is a great deal of difference in methods throughout Spain, and this is nowhere more apparent than in Panadés, where, as in the case of the Torres bodega, the methods are extremely conservative. The process, which I have already mentioned in connection with the Priorato, of oxidizing the wine by exposure in *bombonas* is one of them. It is extremely interesting to see quite a large field of pear-shaped glass bottles, looking for all the world like enormous onions, each of which holds about thirty litres of wine; they have very porous corks and little metal hats so the rain cannot get in. They are surrounded by *bocoyes* of wine, all being matured by direct contact with the elements rather than by the slower process of maturing in the large cool bodegas. The wine stays in its *bombona* for about two years of summer heat and winter rain, when half of it is siphoned off, and the *bombona* is filled with new wine. In other words, this is a kind of open-air solera system on a comparatively small and expensive scale. The resulting wine has a character all its own, and, although it is not sold in Spain (but it is sold everywhere else in the world) and cannot be called Sherry, it has a strong Sherry affinity, though with its own special character, which I must say I rather liked. I am told that there are very few of these fields of *bombonas* left, and by modern standards I suppose this method could hardly be economic or efficient, but I shall deplore its passing. The old fiddle-shaped *bombona*, which held much less than its pear-shaped successor, has now, for all practical purposes, gone out.

In the Torres bodega is blended the wine known as 'Sangre de Toro', or bull's blood, which has nothing to do with the Bull's Blood of Hungary and indeed is a finer wine altogether, of a rich, ruby colour, but

G

not as black as in the Hungarian variety. Again, as in Tarragona, the export wines tend to follow popular demand in that there are *seco* and *semiseco* varieties of white and *semiseco* red wines, with a good clean *rosado* as well. I shall, I think, mention two superb wines, typical of Panadés, that I drink here in England, although they are not easy to come by. These are 'Viña Sol', a clean, dry white wine, and 'Coronas', a very delicious, rather heavy red. But Allah in his wisdom has ordained that the juice of the grape can be purveyed much as the vintner wishes, and Panadés is not exempt from the principle that if wines are blended too much they tend to lose their original character, which is a good thing in some of the less agreeable wines, but it is regrettable in others.

Sitges, on the coast south-east of Villafranca, is noted for its dessert wines. These are made in two types, Malvasía (or Malmsey, as we know it in England) and Moscatel, both of high alcoholic strength and with a high sugar content of up to 9° Baumé. The Malvasía or Malmsey is, of course, made in other countries, and whether the Malmsey in which the Duke of Clarence was drowned came from Sitges, Cyprus, the Canaries, or somewhere else, we do not know. (Incidentally, how did they drown him in a butt of Malmsey? There is only one entrance, and that is through the bung-hole, so they must have cut His Grace up into very small pieces first.) It is generally supposed that the stocks from which the Malvasía grapes are grown were imported from Cyprus by one of the Spanish expeditions to the East in the Middle Ages. Considerable care is needed in the growing of the vines and their grapes, the vintage not taking place until the grape is thoroughly overripe and wrinkled, as in the case of the sweeter Sherries. The wine is kept in vat and cask for a long time, and is normally not bottled for seven or eight years in the best qualities, when it reaches a degree of alcohol of about 16°. The Moscatel of Sitges contains about 15° of alcohol and 9° Baumé, and it has the characteristic taste of all muscatels in that the taste of the grape is predominant. Fermentation is normally stopped at an early stage by the addition of a small amount of grape-alcohol to retain the sweetness, and the more commercial wines are ready for selling after one or two years, during which time they are racked from cask to cask three or four times.

The natural white wine of Panadés appears to be very suitable for distillation into brandy, and two of the best of the Spanish brandies, Mascaro and Torres, are equal, in my opinion, to any of those of Jerez.

The red wines of the Torres bodega are made almost entirely on the Bordeaux system; this is exceptional in Spain. After the first fermentation, the wine is put straight into hogsheads, and it is racked three times during its first year, twice in the second, and once in the third, after which it is clarified with white of egg; it is then ready to be sold, although in practice it may well stay a year or two longer. Here also the best wines are sold as the wine of a given year; this is not necessarily an indication of improvement, because with an equable climate the quality remains firmly constant, but it is an indication of the age of the wine. This bodega has some comparatively old wine, and I was given to drink the Torres 'Coronas' wine of 1941, which was very good, whereas a Bordeaux of that age would certainly not be, and this I think is a good illustration of the difference between the two types of wine.

Probably the most efficient bodega in Panadés is that of the Segura Hermanos, who have one of the most up-to-date plants in Spain – tiles, filters, refrigeration, stainless steel, plastic floors, the lot. Apart from making excellent wine of their own, they specialize in making exactly the right type of basic wine, which is bought by the makers of sparkling wine in the district, to be processed by the *méthode champenoise* and other less reputable ways into sparkling wines.

The delicious wines of Alella must make our next refreshing subject. The *denominación de origen* area of Alella is centred on the small town of the same name about twenty kilometres north of Barcelona just off the coast road, and it is here, if anywhere, that the authentic character of Spanish wine is preserved, to the exclusion of those wines that are blended in the bodegas for marketing to an established pattern laid down by the buying public in other countries. The white wine is made largely from the Garnacha Blanca and Xarello grapes, and the red wine from the Tempranillo and Garnacha Tinta grapes. The vines are grown on a gritty, granite soil that, in itself, is a guarantee that they will not be prolific and that there will be a certain character in the wine. I arrived in the middle of the vintage at the cooperative Alella

Vinícola in the town of Alella, and was able to see the whole process from beginning to end, and eventually to taste and appreciate the wines, for which I have formed a good deal of enthusiasm.

While I was there the carts and trailers and *camiones* were coming in laden with grapes. But in this case the possibly more scientific and less interesting procedure of the tiny wooden balls in Tarragona is not followed; instead, a sample of grapes is pressed at the time of arrival at the weigh-house in a miniature wine-press, in every way a replica of the great wine-presses that have been used for centuries. There are four of these miniature presses in the weigh-house, and, as the loads of grapes arrive, two or three bunches are taken and pressed out on the spot. A sample is whipped upstairs to the laboratory while the grapes are being unloaded into the pressing-chambers opposite, and an analysis is made; the grower is given a tally-check that states the weight of the grapes and their sugar content, according to which he will be paid. I found this operation quite fascinating, particularly in the tiny presses, which are manipulated by hand.

The grapes are shovelled into the press; the stalks are removed, and the grapes are pressed in a series of four pneumatic presses, which ensure that they are not bruised, and that the infusion of excessive tannin from the pips is thus avoided. After this the resulting must is pumped off into fermenting-vats, where it undergoes its first turbulent fermentation. It is then transferred into great oak storage-vats, in which it stays for one or two years, maturing in the wood. No filters are used, nor is alcohol added to fortify the wine, and no wine is ever sold before it is three years old, when it is taken from the enormous oak butts and, normally, bottled both for the domestic and export markets, with the exception of England and Switzerland, where it is shipped in bulk because, as the manager of the cooperative said, he can trust his agents there to bottle it and label it in accordance with the specifications. The wine thus made has both character and charm, two qualities that are difficult to combine. It has a most delicious nose, which reminded me distantly of wallflowers of a gone generation. I am sorry to become poetic, but this faint perfume, too light to be called aromatic, needs some description, for I found it in all the wines I tasted at the bodega.

Half a dozen wines are made under the label 'Alella Legítimo', which speaks for itself; the wines are dated according to the year in which they are made, and this is mainly a true indication of the age of the wine. These wines are the true wines of Alella, where red and white wines are made; they do not compare, nor do they attempt to compare, with the great wines of the Médoc or the Côte d'Or, yet they have a special quality of their own that I found not only attractive but quite remarkable. The white wines do not aspire to be Montrachets or Moselles; they are just straight 'Alella Legítimo', and they are quite delicious.

The range of wines is comparatively small. There are two simple white wines. One is dry, the 'Marfil Seco'; the other, not quite so dry (and it is, I think, a little better), is called 'Marfil Blanco'. They both have about 13° of alcohol. There is also an older white wine called 'Super Marfil'; this, with age, has achieved a more golden colour than its younger brethren, but retains the character of dryness and, above all, the fragrance of this distinctive wine. Further along the line there is a wine called 'Lacre Gualda', which is very old and very dry indeed, of high strength, with a minimum of 17° alcohol, and with a smoothness and fragrance that are altogether exceptional. The red wine, the 'Marfil Tinto', is again strong-bodied, containing 13·5° alcohol, but is smooth and delicate and is typical of that country. A certain amount of sweet wine is made under the name of 'Lacre Violeta'; it is sweet but not cloying, and of a lovely colour, with the characteristic fragrance, but it is essentially a dessert wine. Finally there is a *rosado*, which is a mixture of the juice from white and red grapes and has an alcoholic content of 13°. The colour is a pale terra-cotta; the wine is quite dry, and again it retains the aroma that I find so interesting and charming in the white and red wines.

Wines have been made in Alella since the Roman days, and there are plenty of records from then on to prove it. This is a comparatively small wine-growing area, confined entirely to its gritty soil; the cultivation both of the grape and of the wine itself is highly regulated according to the tradition peculiar to the area. Above all, and to repeat myself, the wines of Alella have preserved the integrity and character of the Spanish wine to a degree that I did not find anywhere else on the Mediterranean littoral, except perhaps in Priorato, and I hope they will long continue to do so.

These wines are not easily come by, for they are relatively expensive, but they are fine wines in every sense of the word and well worth going to a great deal of trouble to find; in fact, one of the best reasons for visiting the Costa Brava might be to look at the wines of Alella. I am greatly indebted to Señor Don José María Vidal, President of the Consejo Regulador of the Denominación de Origen Alella (who believes firmly in the future of Spanish wines, and who took me to Alella), and also to Señores Rifa and Golderila of the cooperative Alella Vinícola. There are, I believe, only two other cooperatives making the wines of Alella in the whole area, and they also preserve the integrity of the wine and do not try to blend or make it into something else.

North of Alella and towards the French frontier there are wine-growing areas that do not come under any *denominación de origen*. In one such area lies Ampurdán, where, under the label of the Barón de Terrades, are made straightforward red and white *vinos de mesa*; they are not particularly distinguished, but they have a character that is essentially Spanish, and they are very good to drink. A sweeter, fortified wine is also made, which is of some character.

At the famous Castillo de Perelada, white, *rosado*, and red wines are made. They are sound wines of excellent quality, and have certain lasting properties, which I know, because I brought a few bottles back with me from my first tour in Spain in 1950 and drank them only two or three years ago, when they had become rather darker but were not only drinkable but excellent. Perelada also make a sparkling wine by the *cuvée close* method; and it is better and rather drier than most of its brethren. These wines are made near the French frontier; all are good examples of their kind.

Inland from Barcelona, in the province of Lérida, the vineyards are comparatively few and far between. An excellent white wine, however, is made in the village of Castell del Remei.

CHAPTER 9

Some Other Wines of Spain

GALICIA

I must confess this province is one of the few areas of Spain to which I have never travelled, and, although I have every intention of going there before very much longer, I cannot claim to be able either to describe the scenery or to give any first-hand information about wines drunk at the bodega. I have, however, drunk of these excellent wines in Madrid and elsewhere, and can commend them as being wines with characters of their own, rather different from those of most Spanish wines, which are inclined to be smooth rather than lively.

Vines are grown generally in this area. The chief wine-growing centre is Ribadavia, not far from Orense and Leiro, although excellent white wines come from Bordones further west. The wines are not exported much, if at all; but they deserve to be, and I hope the day will come when I shall be able to buy them in London. The main characteristic of the white wines is a slight greyness, which is a little off-putting at first – until you taste them; then you find the difference, for they have a freshness and sharpness that makes them comparable with the famous *vinhos verdes* of Portugal, and this is what mostly distinguishes them from the other Spanish wines. The white wines are often sold with their secondary fermentation incomplete, and with the corks stoutly tied on the bottles with string. The wines don't look very nice, being somewhat cloudy, and the bottles, if you carry them about in a car as I did, are liable to explode, which is not a very good thing for the inside

127

of the car. I had three bottles in all, and one went off as described. The other two never got the chance: they were drunk that night. This wine is very good indeed if taken as what it is – an incomplete wine that should be drunk for excitement or interest, or to quench a thirst, or for any purpose other than criticism. When the wine is completed, it is a perfectly well-balanced wine with, as I have said, a character all its own, and with an acerbity that makes a very pleasant change. The alcoholic content is low for Spanish wines, never exceeding 11°, and it is sometimes much lower.

There are many different grapes grown in this region, especially the types that are called Caiño, which are considered the best for bottled wines; other types are Brancellao, Pozeo, Souson, and the Godello or Treizadura, which give fame to those white Galician wines that are called Tostadillo and are similar to the ones that come from near Santander. Another grape, the Albariño, produces very special white wines, Albariño de Meyra and Albariño de Fefiñanes, which are comparable with the German wines, and are highly valued locally.

Sweet wines are made in Galicia, including the celebrated Tostado, which is somewhat similar to Port, and is made by allowing the grapes to dry in the sun and become 'toasted' – hence the name; it contains 14° to 16° of alcohol.

As a wine of this sort is produced, you naturally expect that sparkling wine would be made in Galicia, but, so far as I know, it is not made by the *méthode champenoise*. I have not tasted any of the sparkling wines made by the *méthode cuvée close*, and I hope none are produced by an injection of carbonic acid gas; the wine would certainly deserve a better fate than that.

CASTILE

The wine-producing areas of Castile are centred around Valladolid, and the most important is the village of Rueda (which for a long time has given its name to the wines of that particular district), together with La Seca and Nava del Rey. The wines are very similar to those of the Rioja, but with a slightly higher percentage of alcohol; they are

firm to the palate and have an average alcoholic content of between
13° and 14°. They are white, or rather golden, wines, and they have a
somewhat Sherry-like aroma. They are extremely pleasant to drink.

The impression gained by the traveller across the Castilian plain
from (say) Burgos through Valladolid, Zamora, and Salamanca, is one
of dullness. It is a plain about 2,000 feet high, and it stretches for miles
and miles with nothing to relieve it except the occasional village, with
its statutory three churches and the dovecots, which are a feature of the
landscape. The sun in summer is extremely hot here, and in the winter
the cold can be intense; not exactly, one would say, the best kind of
climate for the making of great wine. Nevertheless some of the Castilian
wines are very good to drink, and are of amazing variety. Most of them
are consumed locally, since they do not travel well, and are consequently little known beyond their centres of production. Even in
Madrid or Bilbao, they are difficult to come by. They have a good reputation, dating back to the sixteenth and seventeenth centuries, when the
wines were fashionable. Most of the wines are white (or *blanco*), but
there are a fair number of light *tinto* wines that are equally agreeable.
From the province of Valladolid comes one of the greatest Spanish
table wines, the 'Vega Sicilia'. The output of this vineyard is very small,
and these wines are difficult to find, even in good restaurants; they are
also expensive by Spanish standards. To a certain extent, they could
be called the Spanish equivalent of the Romanée Conti, although it
would be risky to push this comparison too far.

A little to the west, in the Tierra del Vino, are found the wines from
Zamora and Toro; the vineyards more or less adjoin those round
Tordesillas (which comes under the general Rueda classification), and
have some affinity with them. And yet there is a slight distinction that is
quite interesting; they reach as far as the upper borders of the Douro
before it descends into Portugal. The chief towns of this particular part
of Castile, apart from Zamora and Toro, are Corrales, Benavente,
Fuentesaúco, and Villalpando, and, after reconquest from the Moors,
this region was one of the first organized wine-producing regions of the
newly formed Christian state, when it made part of the territory
belonging to the kings of León. One of these ancient kings once

boasted, '*Tengo un toro que da vino y un león que se lo bebe*', which means 'I have a bull that yields wine and a lion that drinks it' – a very pretty pun on the name Toro, which is the wine-producing town, and the name León, which is the neighbouring city where most of the wine was consumed. These wines are quite robust and agreeable to the palate, and have a comparatively high alcoholic content, of 14° to 15°. They are a deep rich red; sometimes they are called locally *sangre de toro*, or bull's blood (another pun), but I am told that this is now a trade-name owned by the reputable firm of Torres in Villafranca del Panadés, and may not be used on the label. But the wine is still known as bull's blood locally, and this is not a bad name for it.

Further north, around Santander in the Liébana region, the Tosta-dillo wine is produced, which is white, rather sweet, and suitable for a dessert wine. Very good red wines of a rather startling bright colour are produced that have rather a strong character, not at all unpleasant. The wines that come from this area are similar to those to the north of Valladolid, and are either red or dark *rosé*; they have a low alcoholic content but are excellent *vinos corrientes*.

NAVARRE

Navarre is a large province stretching along the foothills of the Pyrenees from rather north of Logroño and through Puente la Reina to Pamplona. The vines are grown sporadically through this very mountainous region, and the wines vary considerably in style and alcoholic strength, for some are of 16° or 18°, while those of Rebea reach up to 15°; by contrast, various wines produced around Pamplona are of only 9° or 10°, but they look much stronger because they have an intense ruby colour.

The scenery of Navarre is very much more dramatic than that of the Rioja near by, with its gentle charm. Apart from Pamplona, which is very much a tourist city, especially during the fiesta week, when the bulls are coursed through the streets, and when much good Navarre wine is drunk, this lovely province is not so much visited by tourists as perhaps it should be. While I have no desire to make it over-popular, I can thoroughly recommend it both for its scenic qualities and for its very pleasant local wines. It is true that something like 3,000,000 litres of Navarre wine were exported in 1964; but this is a very small proportion of the whole, most of it being sold for local consumption – and I cannot blame the locals for choosing their own excellent wine rather than buying from elsewhere in Spain.

The best Navarrese wines I tasted bore the *marque* of Señorío de Sarría from Puente la Reina, about fifteen miles from Pamplona. In addition to its being a very beautiful town indeed, with one of the most magnificent ancient bridges in Europe (marvellously floodlit by night, incidentally), I found its wines fresh and sparkling; and when I say sparkling I do not mean *pétillant* to taste, but with a vivacity uncommon in Spanish wines. I was delighted with this wine; I thought it very pleasant to drink after the heavy dignity of the Riojan giants. The Riojas are the Spanish grandees, and the wine I tasted of the Señorío de Sarría, a *tinto* three years old, was rather like his beautiful and vivacious young bride.

The red wine from Las Campanas, Castillo de Tiebas, is quite remarkable and indeed is comparable with the best Riojas. The *rosé* from Las Campanas is also very good. But all these Navarrese wines are extremely drinkable.

ARAGON

Aragon wine is sometimes known by its principal wine-growing town, Cariñena, but wine is made fairly evenly over the region, which comprises the provinces of Zaragoza, Huesca, and Teruel. It is what I would call average wine of a pleasant character, most of which is drunk locally. Some very good wines are produced in Aragon, especially those made from the Garnacha grape, which accounts for most of the red wine. Some 630,000 litres were exported in 1964, and I imagine most of the wine would go for *coupage*, and possibly for the improvement of worse wines from other countries. In Aragon, the method of wine-making varies a little from that of other districts, for the must is fermented in subterranean wells of a standard size, 3·80 metres (12 ft 5½ in.) deep, 2·80 metres (9 ft 2½ in.) wide, and 2·90 metres (9 ft 6½ in.) long, and a certain amount of treading still goes on, although the modern cooperative has largely made this unnecessary and uneconomical. After the boisterous fermentation, the *bagasse* is extracted, pressed, and sent to the distillery, and the clear wine is racked off into *bocoyes* for finishing. Eventually a rather sweet wine is produced, 15° before fermentation and finishing up as 9° Baumé, both red and white; but it is unlikely that you will find them outside Aragon, where they are drunk young and fresh. I have before me a copy of the publication *Información Comercial Española*, devoted to wine, in which I read: 'The wine of Cariñena, aside from its own excellent value, has the merit of completing the scale of Spanish wines in all its degrees'. Just exactly what this means I am not at all sure, but even so I shall be inclined to agree with it. The wines of Aragon are honest and good, by and large, and convey something of an average of the *vinos corrientes* of Spain.

ESTREMADURA

The wine-growing district of Estremadura lies between Portugal to the west, Huelva to the south, La Mancha to the east, and León to the north; and a great deal of wine is made in this very pleasant province. Its most important one is probably the ill-named Clarete of Guadalcanal. I say ill-named, because it is unnecessary for Spanish wines to bear French names; on the other hand, I have never been quite persuaded that the French have a monopoly of the word 'claret' – certainly they have not of *clarete*. This wine, as its name implies, is a light *rosé*, but with rather more alcoholic content than a true Claret. Many typical wines, both red and white, are produced in Almendralejo, the centre of this region, and the red and white wines of Guareña are also considered excellent. They are no better than those of Salvatierra de los Barros, which are prized locally for their intense colour, and those of Alburquerque, which are reputed to have a distinctive aroma.

The red and white wines of this district are usually extremely well made, and they vary in alcoholic strength from 14° to 17°. The red wines are very brilliant; they also throw a crust, which is unusual in Spanish wine. They have a very similar taste, and when they are very young they are sometimes cloudy. This is largely due, I think, to the fact that they are sold before the secondary fermentation is complete, though they don't appear *pétillant*; it may be that they are not clarified, which is more likely, because it seems possible that the yeasts of the fermentation are similar to the 'flower' formed in Sherry, and have not been properly cleared, as they are in the great bodegas of Jerez. Moreover we must remember the very important difference in the price. Certainly they have a very pleasant nose, and a good clean taste, and there are also some strong-bodied *vinos corrientes* of the Trujillo region that have their admirers.

HUELVA

Sometimes known as the *vinos del Condado de Niebla*, the wines of Huelva now have their own *denominación de origen*, deserving special mention and, so far as this book is capable of it, a word of encouragement, because they have had some very hard luck recently.

Huelva lies north-west of the Guadalquivir river, and the district contains the villages of Moguer, Niebla, Almonte, Villalba del Alcor, Manzanilla (which does not make the wine of that name), and Chucena, together with La Palma del Condado, which is the largest, and Bollulos par del Condado. These wines are generally strong, big wines of fairly high alcoholic content, and sometimes sweet. But they are very suitable for blending; they have thus been very much the victims of circumstance. For, largely owing to its geographical position just north of the Jerez vineyards, the district has, until recently, been able to sell its wines for blending with Sherry at a much higher price than the bodegas would normally be able to get for the *corriente* wine.

Now, however, the winds of change are blowing – and, as far as Huelva is concerned, have blown; for, under the strict limitation of the area in which Jerez wines can be produced and sold as Sherry, the excellent wines of Huelva are just too far away, and they can no longer be used for blending with Sherry, or command such a high price. This is a considerable misfortune, and many deputations have been sent to Madrid to try to get the *denominación de origen* authorities and the Minister of Agriculture to allow the practice to continue, but with no effect; Huelva will therefore have to work out its own future and establish its own reputation. This may be a good thing in the long run; but it is very hard, and it will be very hard for a year or two yet to come, on those growers who have seen their prices chopped in half by one fell stroke of an administrative pen. Such a state of affairs may well give us pause for a little philosophical reflection on why a wine can command a certain price with a certain name, and only half that price when the name is taken away, although without question it is still the same wine.

The Huelva wines (or Niebla wines, as they were sometimes called) have a considerable history. They are made largely by the local growers, and by the careful but fairly primitive methods still used in Jerez and other parts of Spain, although no doubt some bodegas have been modernized and others will be. Wines have been made here from deepest antiquity, and there are records going back to the Moorish occupation; in fact, the last of the petty sultans of Niebla, Mohammed ben Yahya 'Izz ad-Din (1041–51), considered his cellars his greatest treasure, so one assumes that he did not eventually enter paradise, as promised in the Koran. Personally, I should have said it was worth the gamble.

To sum up, the wines of Huelva are both red and white, but mostly white, and these last have a strong affinity with Sherry wine. The demand for Huelva wine is largely because of its importance for *coupage*, and this is probably the fate of the bulk of the 410,000 litres exported last year; but it is much to be hoped that the local growers, under the reverses they have suffered in not being able to sell their wine for blending with Sherry, will do their own blending, and will develop a wine with its own character that will enable them to command a better price.

THE BALEARICS AND THE CANARIES

So far as the wines of Majorca and the Balearics generally are to be met with, they are available only on their own ground (that is, on the islands), and there is little point in writing about them, except to say that I have tasted them here in England, and that they are very good of their sort (mostly white), but never go higher than the simple *vinos corrientes* that are usually good throughout Spain. I have also looked at the wines of Majorca, both red and *rosado*, from the bodega of Jaime Ripoll Benisalem. They are somewhat heavily flavoured, but have an affinity with Valencian and Murcian wines. Their character is, however, quite distinctive. I am not sure whether they can now be bought outside their island of origin. The chief wine of Minorca is the Alba Flora.

The Canaries, however, are in rather a different category; although the wine has a very considerable history, and has been imported into England for many centuries, its character has somewhat changed from what it was originally. As Canary Sack, or just straight Canary, it was always important, and Mistress Quickly in *Henry IV*, Part 2, exclaims, 'That's a marvellous searching wine, and it perfumes the blood ere one can say, "What's this?"' It sounds as though it didn't taste all that good, either. Nevertheless Canary wine was drunk by our Elizabethan forefathers in considerable quantities; but just how it compared with the modern Canary, we shall never know.

Canary wines are made from several types of grapes, but mostly from the Histan white and black, Lolle black, and our dear old friend Pedro Ximénez, without which I think Spain would surely founder. The alcoholic content of these rather dry red and white wines varies between 13° and 15°; in most of the semi-sweet wines, Malvasías and Moscatels, the range is between 15° and 16°, which is normal for Spain. The Malmsey was probably the chief export to Britain in olden days.

Though I have drunk of Canary wines, I have never been to the islands. But I think I should go, if only to find out whether the wines travel well or not. I can think of many worse reasons for going to the Canaries.

CHAPTER 10

The Sparkling Wines of Spain

Nowadays in England it is illegal to speak of Spanish sparkling wine as Champagne, which it most certainly is not, although it is called Champan throughout Spain and in other parts of the world. Sparkling wine is made mainly in the Panadés area, at Perelada near the French frontier, and in the Rioja. These areas have considerably increased their output of sparkling wine during the past few years. The Spanish feel extremely annoyed that they are not allowed to call their sparkling wine Champagne, while the rest of the world produces wine that is similar to Jerez and calls it Sherry; but so the matter goes, and, until the whole question of vinous nomenclature is settled, it will probably continue that way. I do not think I shall live to see the day.

Sparkling wines are made in Spain in three ways: the *méthode champenoise* (at least no one can stop them from using this term for making the wine); the *méthode cuvée close*, where the fermentation is carried out in a vat and thereafter the wine is sold and bottled quite quickly, getting its sparkle from the secondary fermentation; and the execrable method by which carbonic acid gas is introduced into a natural still wine – the results are all horrid and give you the sensation of intoxicating, fizzy, cloyingly sweet lemonade. The Spaniards are not alone in this dubious operation; it is also carried out in France and Germany.

The Spanish Government proposes to control the manufacture of 'Champagne' by stipulating that only the firms who make their sparkling wine by the *méthode champenoise* may describe themselves as *cavas*.

136

Plate 12. Some ancient wine from Tarragona,
sweet and good (*see* Chapter 8)
Kenneth Swain

Consequently, if when visiting Spain you drop in at a *cava* (as, in France, you can drop in on any *cave* and be shown around and be given wine to taste), you may be sure that you will see sparkling wine made as it should be; and I strongly advise you, if you have not already seen it, to do so. It is an extremely complicated and interesting process. It is necessarily also very expensive; hence the high price of Champagne and other wines in other countries made by the same process.

One of the reasons why the name Champagne should not be used in Spain is that the true Champagne comes from the tiny Pinot *noir* and Pinot *blanc* grapes, grown on the very thin and chalky soil of Champagne, which gives the wine that touch of acerbity and crispness which is not found anywhere else in the world. There is no soil in Spain comparable to that of the Champagne district in France, and no Pinot grapes are grown in Spain. Consequently Spanish sparkling wine has quite a different character, a softness that is not found in Champagne. Finally it comes down to a matter of taste. If you like your sparkling wine to have an edge to it (or I suppose one might say more appropriately, with Champagne, a kiss to it), you will buy your Champagne from France; but, if you like your wine soft, you can hardly do better than to try some of the best qualities of Spanish sparkling wine.

Sparkling wine in Spain, as indeed in France, can be brought to almost any degree of sweetness; this is purely a matter of the amount of *liqueur* that is added at the time of *dégorgement*. I think in this case I have to use the French terms, because they are more readily understood; but perhaps it would be better if I explained the complicated *méthode champenoise* process undergone by sparkling wine before it reaches the end for which it was ordained, whether it be a wedding breakfast or a chorus girl's slipper, or just to make a good wine for you and for me to drink with or before our dinner.

First of all, the grapes are pressed carefully in such a way that the pips will not be bruised and let tannin into the wine, making it bitter. Sparkling wine, which ought to be white or very pale gold, can be made from either white or black grapes, and in Champagne it is made from both. In Spain most of the sparkling wine is made from white grapes; it is what the French would call *blanc de blanc*. If black grapes are used in

H

making the wine, the skins are removed from the must before fermentation begins, because it is the pigment from the skins of the grapes that makes the wine red. After pressing, the must can be pumped directly into casks; more often it is pumped into vats for not more than a day to allow the must to settle, and then, before fermentation sets in, the comparatively clear juice is pumped into barrels, where it undergoes its first tumultuous fermentation. While this is going on, if you put your ear to the bung-hole, which is always open, you can hear the wine inside buzzing like a swarm of angry bees. The wine is left in the cask for between six months and a year, but, before the secondary fermentation is finished, it is clarified and blended in a blending-tank to make the wine of an even quality. This blended wine, called the *cuvée*, is bottled with small amounts of sugar and yeast and corked with temporary corks, and it starts its long ageing in the cellars deep below the earth.

There, lying horizontally in vast bins, these hundreds of thousands of bottles stay with nothing happening at all to them for at least three years, and sometimes longer. After this time, they are put in specially made racks, bottom-upward at an angle of 45°, and every day the bottles are given a kind of shake and quarter-turn to send the sediment, the crust that has grown into the wine, to the bottom. This is an extremely expert job, and there are men who do nothing but turn the wine, two bottles at a time, at incredible speed; over the years, they develop enormous muscles in the forearms. This process of turning takes about six months. (At this stage, for the cheaper wine, the bottle can go through its *dégorgement* and be ready to drink; but this is not usual.) The bottles are then placed upside-down, so that the shaken-up sediment will collect at the end of the cork; and there they stay for any period. I know that there is a bin of wine in the upside-down position in Epernay that has been there for fifty years without *dégorgement*; for all I know, there may be some similar in Spain.

The wine is now ready for finishing. When they are required, the bottles will be put on specially prepared trolleys with racks, still in the upside-down position, and taken along and put into a machine that freezes the wine solid in the neck of the bottle. Then follows the *dégorgement*, which is the removal of the temporary cork and of the frozen sediment that has accumulated over the years. The *liqueur* is added to the clear wine to give it the necessary degree of sweetness, ranging from 0·05 per cent of *liqueur* for a *brut* or dry wine, to 4 or 5 per cent for our South American friends who like their sparkling wine sweet as well as good – and 4 or 5 per cent of *liqueur* can make the wine pretty sweet. The *liqueur* is, in fact, grape-sugar. Then the wine is corked with its final cork and wired down; the bottle is washed (and it needs washing after all those years in a cellar), labelled, and sent on its way. The wine will not improve in bottle; indeed, it will deteriorate, and only very well-made sparkling wine of a very good year will sparkle much after about ten years. In Spain, where the years do not vary, the wine will become flat or still, the sparkle will disappear, and the colour will darken. I personally happen to like old Champagne, but it is not by any means to everybody's taste. Certainly it is not the kind of thing you expect if you buy a bottle of sparkling wine at a high price.

So, from all this, we can appreciate that Champagne is, and must be, a comparatively expensive product. In the whole of Spain there are about forty firms making wine by the *méthode champenoise*, and more making wine by the *méthode cuvée close* and, alas! by injecting carbonic acid gas.

The *cuvée close* method is certainly not harmful, but it constitutes an artificial acceleration of a purely natural process, and the wine is sometimes drinkable, as can be seen; but it cannot compare with the long and intricate *méthode champenoise*. It is perhaps unfortunate for the Spanish that, when the famous 'Spanish Champagne case' was fought out in the English courts, the firm who were the Spanish defendants were making their sparkling wine by the *méthode cuvée close*.

I have been taken over the great Codorníu sparkling-wine bodega in San Sadurní de Noya by Señor Don José María Raventós, whose family has been making wine there since 1551, long before Dom Pérignon discovered the art of making Champagne. In those days, of course, the Codorníu family made wine as everybody else did, probably a better wine, but just straight wine. In the nineteenth century, however, having tasted the wine of Champagne and made some experiments of their own, they found that the grapes of Panadés were very suitable for the production of sparkling wine, and they tried it out in a small way; this was in 1872, when Don José Raventós produced his first bottles of sparkling wine. Now Codorníu make their wine in several qualities, the best being a very dry wine called 'Non Plus Ultra', which is certainly the best Spanish sparkling wine I have tasted. Moreover these vast cellars – which, I am informed, are nearly twice as large as any other cellars in the world (and I was surprised to hear this) – are visited every year by some 80,000 tourists, Spanish and foreign, who may be sure of a most interesting visit and a glass of excellent sparkling wine at the end of it.

There are many *cavas* in the Panadés district, and San Sadurní de Noya in particular, that will welcome the casual visitor and refresh him with a glass of very good sparkling wine. Remember that only those firms making their sparkling wine by the *méthode champenoise* can describe themselves as *cavas*. On your way to the Costa Blanca, the Costa del Sol, or any point south, do not be afraid to visit – indeed, you should make a point of visiting – a *cava*. You will spend a worthwhile hour or so before you go on your way refreshed.

CHAPTER II

Spanish Brandy

Brandy is distilled throughout the length and breadth of Spain, and it varies enormously in quality. In Spain it sometimes appears under the label Coñac, which is a pity, because it is nothing like Cognac, and it gives an impression that Spanish brandy is trying to pass itself off as its French elder brother – or rather half-brother, because the two are not really alike except in their method of manufacture. Furthermore Spanish brandy is comparatively young, whereas the brandies of Cognac are extremely old, and this point is very important in the making of brandy. Brandy is in fact distilled wine, and wine must be defined as the fermented juice of the grape. The word 'brandy' derives from the Dutch *brandewijn*, or burnt wine, and this is really what it is, because the wine from which it is made is burnt or boiled until the alcohol, which becomes a gas at many degrees of heat below that of water, is given off. This is then cooled and liquefied and becomes the clear white spirit that is called brandy. Something like ten measures of wine are used to make one measure of brandy, so it is comparatively expensive and should command a much higher price. This is one of the things I have rarely understood in my travels in Spain: that a very good Spanish brandy is hardly dearer than wine.

In the making of brandy, a great deal depends on the quality of the wine from which it is distilled, which in turn depends on the quality of the grapes from which the wine is made. The Cognac of France is distilled from a grape called the St Emilion; this is not remarkable

in itself and does not make a particularly delicious wine, but it has in-
herent qualities that render the brandy distilled from it quite superb.
In Spain, the brandy is distilled from the grapes of the country, whatever they may be and wherever they may be bought; and I should not
be surprised if the very cheapest odd lots of grapes were used for this
purpose, for we must face at once the fact that a great deal of the local
Spanish brandies are not worth drinking. There are, however, some
good brandies up and down the country, and one or two that are truly
excellent. But they are rare birds, and the *coñac corriente* is really fit only
for what it is mostly served for: to put into coffee on a cold morning.

The main difference between the French and Spanish brandies is
that the Spanish ones are sweeter and, by and large, softer. There is
nothing against this, and I believe there is a growing market in England
for a Spanish brandy that, in its better bottles, I would have no hesita-
tion in drinking myself; indeed, I sometimes do drink it. The factor that
is most likely to stop Spanish brandy from rising to the utmost heights is
the enormous quantity that is consumed in Spain, which precludes the
distiller from building up those soleras (to use the Spanish term) of
brandy that are absolutely necessary if it is ever to be great. I believe
Spain would have less difficulty in producing the really great brandy
than the really great wine, because some of the hundreds of varieties of
grapes grown in Spain have an affinity with the St Emilion grape, and,
in the case of brandy, the process is to some extent a mechanical one
and is not so subject to the human element. I am perfectly well aware
that there are many who would disagree with me, but I repeat that I
see no reason why the really great Spanish brandy should not be made
in the future, if an enterprising distiller would work for fifty years or so
to build up his old casks; the cask plays a great part in the development
of fine brandy – as, of course, it does in wine. The casks must be oak of
the best quality, and the brandy when it is made must be left for a long,
long time.

In the enormous cellars in Cognac, big distillers have what they
sometimes call their 'paradise', where are kept the very oldest brandies,
which are never sold and are rarely refreshed; the brandy taken from
them is used to give a distinctive character to the somewhat younger

brandy that is put out under the most famous *marques*. I am aware that most of the brandy-distillers in Spain also have a 'paradise' of this sort, but, since the brandy industry really started in Spain only about eighty years ago and immense quantities have been sold ever since, I doubt very much whether these terribly important stocks have accumulated; I have not found much trace of them in the brandy. After being kept in cask for a hundred years or more, brandy loses strength very rapidly, and the custom in France is to pour it into stone jars and seal it after it gets below about 40° of alcohol. I have tasted such brandy; it is soft and smooth and quite delicious. It is, of course, lifeless; but when mixed with a younger brandy it imparts to it a magnificent character. Brandy once bottled does not improve, so the whole of the maturing process must take place in wood. This is why, when you occasionally see a very dusty bottle with the Napoleonic seal on it and a date like 1811, you know it must be false. If the brandy were truly of 1811 and had been kept in a bottle, it would still be much as it was then, or certainly no better; and, if it had been kept in wood and bottled since, it would be so weak as hardly to be worth drinking.

My personal favourite among Spanish brandies is called 'Mascaro'; it is made in the Panadés district, which also produces the very good 'Torres' brandy. Of course the big Sherry houses put out standard brandies like 'Veterano' and 'Fundador'. They are very even, and, within their limits, their quality is good.

A list of Spanish brandy exporters will be found in Appendix 4.

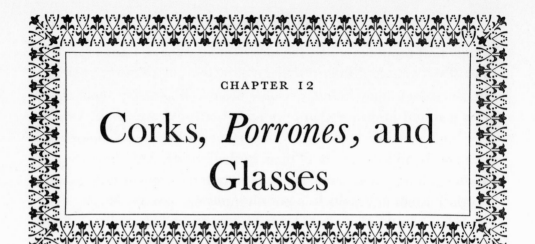

CHAPTER 12

Corks, *Porrones*, and Glasses

There is no lack of excellent cork in Spain, and, if you motor from Lisbon to Seville, on both sides of the frontier you will travel long distances through cork-oak forests interspersed with sweet chestnuts, under which brown, lean, long-haired swine graze in enormous herds. These cork-oak forests are extremely picturesque. The bark is stripped from the oak in sections; underneath, the natural wood is a rich browny-red, giving a most extraordinary appearance to the tree. The stripped cork may be seen in vast dumps at occasional clearings in the forest; it is left there for seasoning before being taken away to cork factories.

In Spain, however, the cork is not of tremendous importance to the wine, because this is almost invariably drunk young, and therefore the corks are short, except in some of the great Riojan vineyards, where the corks used are of the French type that is more than two inches long; in these parts, wine is sometimes kept to a great age, and the cork is correspondingly more important. The function of the cork is not only to stop the wine from coming out of the bottle, but also to stop impurities from going in – because all those microscopic organisms that turn wine into vinegar usually go in through the front door (that is, the cork) from the atmosphere outside; thus, according to the quality of the cork, so the wine will be preserved. In Jerez, even the oldest wines are never kept in bottle, and one may expect to find quite a short cork in a bottle containing Sherry from an 1819 solera. The reason for this has already been explained, but it is only extremely rarely that the wine is bottled and kept in this way. Most of the Spanish wines you buy in England or abroad will naturally have corks supplied in the country where they were bottled, and they will tend to be rather larger and perhaps better corks than those provided by the Spanish bottlers.

Decanters in Spain follow the form of those found elsewhere, but the typical Spanish wine-container is the *porrón*, which is found throughout the country, but especially in Catalonia, where it is in general use. The object of the *porrón* could be, I suppose, merely to save washing up, for no glass is necessary. Wine is poured from the cask into the pear-shaped glass decanter through a curved funnel that is also the handle; in use, it is tipped, sometimes at arm's length, and the wine emerges in a single stream through the spout, directly into the mouth. Normally (and in Catalonia especially) restaurants and working-class families have a *porrón* of wine standing in the middle of the table; the diners reach for it when they want a drink, then put it back. As the spout never touches the lips, there is no need for glasses. Drinking from a *porrón* is something of a skill, which I have never achieved, although I have tried more than once – disastrously.

Because the *porrón* is in common use everywhere, really ancient ones are comparatively few, by reason of their natural fragility. There are, however, some very old and beautiful *porrones* in the Museum of Vini-culture in Villafranca del Panadés.

The traditional glasses of Spain are tulip-shaped and very simple, with the slightest curve outwards at the top. They can be found in good, medium, and indifferent qualities throughout the country. There are not, as in France, characteristic glasses for different regional wines, except in Jerez, where the rather beautiful *copita* or tasting-glass is in general use. This is made in two or three sizes. Thus the smaller ones can be used for *finos* and the larger glasses kept for the fine *amontillados* or *olorosos* that have developed a special bouquet through age. In tasting, these are usually held by the foot of the glass rather than by the stem.

The glasses and *porrón* shown in the drawing on page 149 are all typical of their class, though naturally there are many variants, and sparkling wine is usually, alas! drunk out of what is generally known as a Champagne glass, though it is nothing of the kind; I mean the flat-bottomed glass best calculated to disperse the liveliness of the wine in no time at all. The general attitude of the Spanish to their glasses and so on reflects their attitude to wine in general: it is an agreeable necessity of life, but it is not a religion. This, I suppose, accounts for the fact that French glasses are so very much better, generally, than the Spanish ones. There is no doubt that nothing in Spain can compare, for instance, with the beautiful glasses from Baccarat.

A *porrón* (a), and some typical Spanish wine-glasses: (b) one commonly used throughout Spain for table wine; (c) a Sherry *copita* for *finos*; (d) a larger type for tasting *olorosos* and old *amontillados*; (e) a straight glass used for brandy in the bars of Madrid and elsewhere, and also for table wine and Sherry

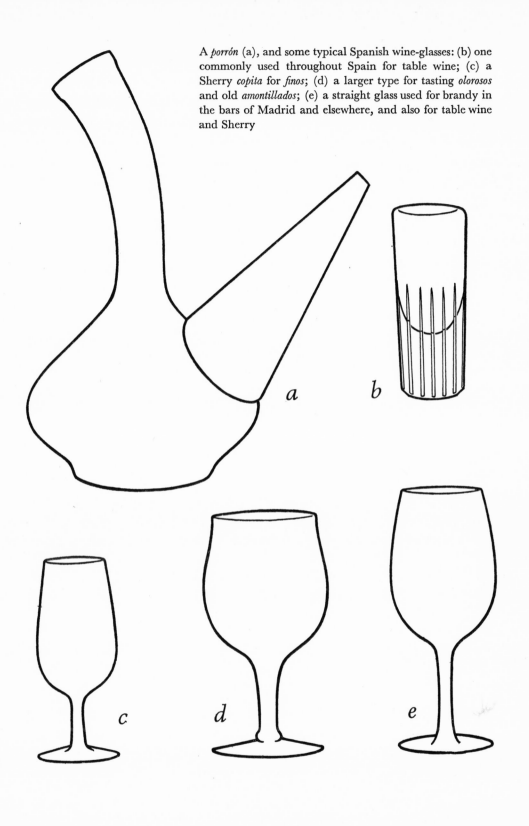

a

b

c

d

e

GRAPES AND WINES OF SPAIN AND
THEIR PLACES OF ORIGIN

I do not think that a complete list of Spanish wines has ever been compiled and codified. So far as such a task is possible, this appendix attempts it. From the tremendous list of wines, the reader will gather much information about the number of them made in Spain and the places where the grapes are grown; in the course of a normal lifetime one would expect to taste very few Spanish wines. Many will never be sold further away than the next large town or city; others have a world-wide reputation. One thing is certain: you will never be too far away from good wine in Spain. For the purposes of this appendix the arrangement is as follows:

In the first column, the names of the principal wine-producing areas are printed in capitals. Each of these areas has a regulating council (*consejo regulador*) that controls the quality of the wines produced within it and the use of its name (or *denominación de origen*). These wines are described in the second column. The name of a village or town in one of these areas (printed in upper- and lower-case Roman) usually has a cross-reference to the *denominación de origen* under which its wines are marketed. Thus, if you wish to know the types of wine produced in the village of Aguarón, you must turn to CARIÑENA, as the wines of Aguarón are marketed under this name.

If the wines of a certain village do not come under any *denominación de origen*, they are described, as far as possible, in the second column, beside the name of the village (also printed in upper- and lower-case Roman). Wines are frequently called after their place of origin. One could therefore say 'Abanilla is a red wine', or one could speak of the 'red wine of Abanilla'.

A wine that has a particular (and often well-known) name is printed in inverted commas (e.g., 'Chacolí', 'Fondillon'), with its description in the second column. The names of grapes, which are frequently applied also to the wines produced from them, are printed in italics, with their colour (whether black or white) shown in the second column.

In the third column are shown the names of the provinces included in the area of a *denominación de origen* (e.g., RIOJA covers the province of Logroño and parts of Navarre, Alava, and Burgos); the province in which a town or village is situated; or the main provinces in which a type of grape is produced.

In the fourth column is noted, where applicable, the *denominación de origen* of the wines of a town or village.

Abbreviations

a/c, alcohol content. esp., especially. ord., ordinary, or common, wine. usu., usually.

NAME	DESCRIPTION			PROVINCE	DENOMINA-CION DE ORIGEN
Abanilla	red	semi-sweet	strong	Murcia	
	(becoming drier with age)				
Abrera	white	dry	low a/c	Barcelona	
Acebo	red	dry	ord.	Cáceres	
Agost	*See* ALICANTE			Alicante	Alicante
Aguarón	*See* CARIÑENA			Zaragoza	Cariñena
Aguilar de la Frontera	*See* MONTILLA			Córdoba	Montilla-Moriles
Agulló	white		sparkling		
Aiguamurcia	*See* PANADES, Central			Tarragona	Panadés
Airen	white			Albacete	
				Ciudad Real	
				Cuenca	
				Toledo	
Alaejos	white	dry	medium a/c	Valladolid	
	clarete	dry	strong		
	red	dry	ord.		
Alameda de la Sagra	*See* MANCHA			Toledo	Mancha
Also 'Moscatel'	white	sweet			
Alarije	white			Badajoz	
Alaró	white	sweet		Balearics	
(Majorca)	red	sweet			
Alba	white			Santander	
Albacete	white		ord.	Albacete	
	dark red	dry	ord.		
Albaflor (Minorca)	white	sweet		Balearics	
Albaida	*See* VALENCIA			Valencia	Valencia
	esp. white	light	table		
Albarín	black			Oviedo	
Albariño	white			Orense	
Albarracín	*See* Aragon			Teruel	
Alberique	*See* VALENCIA			Valencia	Valencia
	esp. white	light	table		
Albillo blanco	white			Avila	
				Cádiz	
				Las Palmas (Canary Is.)	
				Salamanca	
				Santa Cruz de Tenerife (Canary Is.)	
				Valladolid	

NAME	DESCRIPTION			PROVINCE	DENOMINA-CION DE ORIGEN
Albiñana	*See* PANADES, Lower			Tarragona	Panadés
Albuñol	white	sweet	strong	Granada	
Alburquerque	white		ord., medium a/c	Badajoz	
Alcalá de Chivert	red			Castellón de la Plana	
Alcalá la Real	white			Jaén	
Alcázar de San Juan	*See* MANCHA			Ciudad Real	Mancha
Alcorisa	*See* Aragon			Teruel	
Aldeanueva de Ebro	*See* RIOJA			Logroño	Rioja (Baja)
	esp. red	dry	strong		
Aldeanueva del Camino	red	dry		Cáceres	
ALELLA	white	dry	old, strong	Barcelona	Allella
	white	dry	old		
	white	dry			
	white	semi-dry	strong		
	rosado	dry			
	red	dry	strong		
	red	sweet	strong		
Alfamén	*See* CARIÑENA			Zaragoza	Cariñena
Alfaro	*See* RIOJA			Logroño	Rioja (Baja)
	esp. red	dry	strong		
Algarrobo	*See* MALAGA			Málaga	Málaga
ALICANTE	white		ord.	Alicante	Alicante
	white	sweet	high a/c		
	rosado	dry	ord.		
	rosado	dry	fine, table		
	red	dry	ord.		
	red	sweet			
'Alicante'	white	sweet		Alicante	Alicante
	red	sweet			
Aljarafe, El (district)	*clarete*	semi-sweet		Seville	
Almagro	*See* MANCHA			Ciudad Real	Mancha
	esp. red		ord.		
Almansa	*clarete*	dry	high a/c	Albacete	
Almendralejo	white		ord., medium a/c	Badajoz	
	red				
Almonte	*See* HUELVA			Huelva	Huelva
Alora	*See* MALAGA			Málaga	Málaga
Alpera	*clarete*	dry	high a/c	Albacete	
Amandi	red	acrid	ord.	Lugo	
'Amontillado'	*See* SHERRY			Cádiz	Jerez-Xérès-Sherry
Andújar	white	sweet		Jaén	
Añina	*See* SHERRY			Cádiz	Jerez-Xérès-Sherry
	esp. 'Fino', 'Pedro Ximénez'				
Anna	*See* VALENCIA			Valencia	Valencia
	esp. red	light	table		

NAME	DESCRIPTION			PROVINCE	DENOMINA-CION DE ORIGEN
Añover de Tajo Also 'Moscatel'	*See* MANCHA white	sweet		Toledo	Mancha
Antequera	*See* MALAGA			Málaga	Málaga
Aragon (large wine-producing region)	white *rosado* red	acrid	ord. high a/c	Huesca Teruel Zaragoza	
Aranda de Duero	red	dry	ord.	Burgos	
Archidona	*See* MALAGA			Málaga	Málaga
Arcos de la Frontera	white	dry		Cádiz	
Arenas	*See* MALAGA			Málaga	Málaga
Arenas de San Pedro	red		ord.	Avila	
Argamasilla de Alba	*See* MANCHA			Ciudad Real	Mancha
Arganda	red		ord., very high a/c	Madrid	
Arganza	*See* VALDEORRAS			León	Valdeorras
Argentona	white		low a/c	Barcelona	
Arnedo	*See* RIOJA			Logroño	Rioja (Alta)
Arnoya	*See* RIBERO			Orense	Ribero
Arroyo de la Luz	white red	dry	ord., medium a/c	Cáceres	
Artajona	white red	dry dry	light low a/c	Navarre	Navarra
Artés	white	dry	coarse	Barcelona	
Ascó	*See* TARRAGONA			Tarragona	Tarragona
Autol	*See* RIOJA esp. red	dry	strong	Logroño	Rioja (Baja)
Avila	white	dry	rich	Avila	
Avinyó	white	dry	low a/c	Barcelona	
Ayelo de Malferit	*See* VALENCIA esp. red	light	table	Valencia	Valencia
Ayerbe	*See* Aragon			Huesca	
Badajoz	white *clarete*	dry dry	ord. high a/c	Badajoz	
Baena	*See* MONTILLA			Córdoba	Montilla-Moriles
Baeza	*clarete* red			Jaén	
Báguena	*See* Aragon			Teruel	
Baladí	white			Córdoba	
Balbaina	*See* SHERRY esp. 'fino', 'Pedro Ximénez'			Cádiz	Jerez-Xérès-Sherry
Bañeza, La	red	dry	acrid	León	
Baños de Fitero	red	dry	strong	Navarre	Navarra

Plates 13, 14. Two distinctive vineyards: *above*, at Monasterio de Poblet, Tarragona (*see* Chapter 8); *below*, near Valdepeñas (*see* Chapter 5)

Kenneth Swain

NAME	DESCRIPTION			PROVINCE	DENOMINACION DE ORIGEN
Baños de Montemayor	red	dry		Cáceres	
Barbará	*See* Conca de Barbará			Tarragona	
Barbastro	*See* Aragon			Huesca	
Barco de Valdeorras, El	*See* VALDEORRAS			Orense	Valdeorras
Batista	black			Balearics	
Baza	red			Granada	
Begas	*See* PANADES, Central			Barcelona	Panadés
Belchite	*See* Aragon			Zaragoza	
Bellmunt de Giurana	*See* PRIORATO			Tarragona	Priorato
Belmonte	*See* MANCHA			Cuenca	Mancha
Also 'Vinillo Belmontino'	white	light			
Belmonte de Calatayud	red		ord., strong	Zaragoza	
Benabarre	*See* Aragon			Huesca	
Benavente	*clarete*	dry	fine	Zamora	
	red	dry	strong		
Benejama	*See* ALICANTE			Alicante	Alicante
Benicarló	dark red	rich	strong	Castellón de la Plana	
Benicasim	red		high a/c	Castellón de la Plana	
Beniganim	*See* VALENCIA			Valencia	Valencia
	esp. white	light	table		
Benisa	*See* ALICANTE			Alicante	Alicante
Benisalem	white	sweet		Balearics	
(Majorca)	red	sweet			
Berdellos	white			Orense Pontevedra	
Beriain	red	dry	low a/c	Navarre	Navarra
Berlanga de Duero	red	dry	ord.	Soria	
Biar	*See* ALICANTE			Alicante	Alicante
Bisbal del Panadés	*See* PANADES, Central			Tarragona	Panadés
Bobal	black			Albacete Cuenca Valencia	
Bolea	*See* Aragon			Huesca	
Bollullos de la Mitación	usu. white	sweet	strong	Seville	
Bollullos par del Condado	*See* HUELVA			Huelva	Huelva
Bonares	*See* HUELVA			Huelva	Huelva
Bonete	*clarete*	dry	high a/c	Albacete	
Borba	white			Badajoz	
Bordones	white	dry	light	Pontevedra	
Borja 'Moscatel'	dark golden	sweet		Zaragoza	
Bormujos	usu. white	sweet	strong	Seville	

NAME	DESCRIPTION			PROVINCE	DENOMINA-CION DE ORIGEN
Borriol	red		high a/c	Castellón de la Plana	
Briñas	*See* RIOJA			Alava	Rioja (Alavesa)
	esp. red	semi-sweet	light		
Brozas, Las	white		ord., medium a/c	Cáceres	
	red	dry			
Bullas	red	semi-sweet	strong	Murcia	
	(becoming drier with age)				
Buñol	*See* CHESTE			Valencia	Cheste
	esp. white	light	table		
Burbáguena	*See* Aragon			Teruel	
Burjasot	*See* VALENCIA			Valencia	Valencia
Cabezón	red	dry	ord.	Valladolid	
Cabezuela del Valle	red	dry	ord.	Cáceres	
Cabra	*See* MORILES			Córdoba	Montilla-Moriles
Cabrera	*See* PANADES, Upper			Barcelona	Panadés
Cacabelos	*See* VALDEORRAS			León	Valdeorras
Cadaqués	white	sweet		Gerona	
	red				
Cádiz	*See* SHERRY			Cádiz	
Caiño	black			Orense Pontevedra	
Calagraño	white			Logroño	
Calahorra	*See* RIOJA			Logroño	Rioja (Baja)
	esp. red	dry	strong		
Calanda 'Malvasía'	white	sweet		Teruel	
Calatayud	red		ord., strong	Zaragoza	
Caldas de Mombúy	white	dry		Barcelona	
Caldetas	white	dry	light	Pontevedra	
	red	dry			
Cálig	red			Castellón de la Plana	
Cambados	red	acrid	thick	Pontevedra	
Campanas, Las	*clarete*	dry	high a/c	Navarre	Navarra
	red	light	medium a/c		
Campillos	*See* MALAGA			Málaga	Málaga
Campo de Criptana	*See* MANCHA			Ciudad Real	Mancha
Camporrobles	*See* UTIEL			Valencia	Utiel-Requena
Canacazo	white			Cádiz	
Cañamero	white		ord., medium a/c	Cáceres	
	red	dry			

NAME	DESCRIPTION			PROVINCE	DENOMINA-CION DE ORIGEN
Candamo	red	dry		Oviedo	
Canillas 'Moscatel'	golden	sweet		Madrid	
Cañizo	*clarete*	dry	fine	Zamora	
	dark red	dry	strong		
Cantalapiedra	white	dry		Salamanca	
Cantalpino	white	dry		Salamanca	
Capsanes	*See* TARRAGONA			Tarragona	Tarragona
	esp. red	sweet	high a/c		
Caravaca	red	semi-sweet	strong	Murcia	
	(becoming drier with age)				
Carballino	*See* RIBERO			Orense	Ribero
CARIÑENA	white	sweet	fortified	Zaragoza	Cariñena
	clarete	dry	high a/c		
	red		ord., high a/c		
'Pajarilla'	white	sweet			
'Cariñena'	red	sweet	high a/c		
Cariñena	black			Gerona	
				Tarragona	
				Zaragoza	
Carlet	*See* VALENCIA			Valencia	Valencia
'Carlón'	dark red	sweet	rich	Valencia	
Carrascal	*See* SHERRY			Cádiz	Jerez-Xérès-Sherry
	esp. 'Oloroso'				
Carrasquín	black			Oviedo	
Cartaya	*See* HUELVA			Huelva	Huelva
Cartuja de Porta-Celi	red	sweet	rich	Valencia	Valencia
'Moscatel'	white	sweet			
Cartuja de Scala Dei	*See* PRIORATO			Tarragona	Priorato
	esp. white	sweet			
Casas de Benítez	*See* MANCHA			Cuenca	Mancha
	esp. red		strong		
Casas de Haro	*See* MANCHA			Cuenca	Mancha
	esp. red		strong		
Casas Ibáñez	*See* MANCHA			Albacete	Mancha
Cascante	red	dry	medium a/c	Navarre	Navarra
Casetas	*See* Aragon			Zaragoza	
Casinos	*See* VALENCIA			Valencia	Valencia
	esp. white wines				
Castalla	*See* ALICANTE			Alicante	Alicante
Castell del Remei	white			Lérida	
Castellote	*See* Aragon			Teruel	
Castellví de la Marca (Barcelona)	*See* PANADES			Barcelona	Panadés
Castelnou	*See* Aragon			Teruel	
Castilleja de Guzmán	white	sweet		Seville	
Castillo de Locubin	white			Jaén	

NAME	DESCRIPTION			PROVINCE	DENOMINA-CION DE ORIGEN
Castillo de Perelada	*See* Perelada				
Castrelo del Miño	*See* RIBERO			Orense	Ribero
Castro del Río	*See* MONTILLA			Córdoba	Montilla-Moriles
Castro Urdiales				Santander	
'Chacolí'	white	acrid	low a/c		
	and red	acrid	low a/c		
Caudete	*clarete*	dry	high a/c	Albacete	
Caudete de las Fuentes	*See* UTIEL			Valencia	Utiel-Requena
Cavideña	red				
Cayetana	white			Badajoz Cáceres	
Cazalla de la Sierra	white red	light sweet		Seville	
Cebreros	white red	sweet	high a/c ord.	Avila	
Ceclavín	white *clarete*	dry		Cáceres	
Cencibel	black			Mancha	
Cenicero	*See* RIOJA			Logroño	Rioja (Alta)
Cepeda	dark red	dry		Salamanca	
Cervera del Río Alhama	*See* RIOJA esp. red	dry	strong	Logroño	Rioja (Baja)
'Chacolí'	white or red	dry dry	low a/c low a/c	Navarre Santander	
Chapinería					Madrid
'Clarete del Santo'	pale *clarete*	semi-sweet			
CHESTE	white white *rosado* red red	semi-dry sweet dry sweet	light, table light, table table high a/c	Valencia	Cheste
Chiclana de la Frontera	*See* SHERRY			Cádiz	Jerez-Xérès-Sherry
Chinchón	red		ord., very high a/c	Madrid	
Chipiona	*See* SHERRY esp. 'Moscatel'			Cádiz	Jerez-Xérès-Sherry
Chiva	*See* CHESTE			Valencia	Cheste
Chucena	*See* HUELVA			Huelva	Huelva
Cieza	*See* JUMILLA			Murcia	Jumilla
Cigales	white	dry	strong	Valladolid	
Cilleros	*clarete* red	dry dry	ord.	Cáceres	
Cinco Casas	*See* MANCHA			Ciudad Real	Mancha
Cinco Villas, Las (district)	*See* Aragon			Zaragoza	
Cintruénigo	dark red	dry	strong	Navarre	Navarra

NAME	DESCRIPTION			PROVINCE	DENOMINA-CION DE ORIGEN
Cirauqui	red	dry	table, low a/c	Navarre	Navarra
Clariana	white	dry		Lérida	
Coín	*See* MALAGA			Málaga	Málaga
Collet	black			Balearics	
Colmenar	*See* MALAGA			Málaga	Málaga
Colmenar de Oreja	red		ord., very high a/c	Madrid	
Cómpeta	*See* MALAGA			Málaga	Málaga
Conca de Barbará	white	semi-dry	low a/c	Tarragona	
	red	semi-dry	low a/c		
Concha	*clarete*	dry	low a/c	Vizcaya	
Conil de la Frontera	white			Cádiz	
Constantina	white		light	Seville	
	clarete	semi-sweet			
Consuegra	*See* MANCHA			Toledo	Mancha
Córdoba	*See* MONTILLA			Córdoba	Montilla-Moriles
Cordovín	*See* RIOJA			Logroño	Rioja (Alta)
Corella	dark red	dry	strong	Navarre	Navarra
Cornudella	*See* PRIORATO			Tarragona	Priorato
Corrales	*clarete*	dry	fine	Zamora	
	dark red	dry	strong		
Cosuenda	*See* CARIÑENA			Zaragoza	Cariñena
Also 'Garnacha'	red	sweet			
Creixell	*See* PANADES, Lower			Tarragona	Panadés
Cretas	*See* Aragon			Teruel	
Cripán	*See* RIOJA			Alava	Rioja (Alavesa)
'Cuarte'	*clarete*	semi-dry	light, table	Valencia	Valencia
Cubo del Tierra del Vino, El	*clarete*	dry	fine	Zamora	
	dark red	dry	strong		
Cuevas de San Marcos	*See* MALAGA			Málaga	Málaga
Curiel	red	dry	ord.	Valladolid	
Cuzcurrita	*See* RIOJA			Logroño	Rioja (Alta)
Daimiel	*See* MANCHA			Ciudad Real	Mancha
Damós	*See* TARRAGONA			Tarragona	Tarragona
	esp. red	sweet	high a/c		
Daroca	*See* Aragon			Zaragoza	
Doña Mencía	*See* MONTILLA			Córdoba	Montilla-Moriles
Dueñas	*clarete*	dry	fine	Palencia	
	red	dry	ord.		
Ecija 'Perojiménez'	white	sweet		Seville	

NAME	DESCRIPTION			PROVINCE	DENOMINA-CION DE ORIGEN
Elche	*See* ALICANTE			Alicante	Alicante
Elciego	*See* RIOJA			Alava	Rioja (Alavesa)
Elda	*See* ALICANTE			Alicante	Alicante
Elvillar	*See* RIOJA			Alava	Rioja (Alavesa)
Encinacorba	*See* CARIÑENA			Zaragoza	Cariñena
Enguera	*See* VALENCIA esp. red wines			Valencia	Valencia
Epila	*See* Aragon			Zaragoza	
Escalona	*See* MANCHA esp. red wines			Toledo	Mancha
Espartinas	usu. white	sweet	strong	Seville	
Espolla	red	sweet	high a/c	Gerona	
Esquivias	*See* MANCHA			Toledo	Mancha
Estella	*clarete*	dry	low a/c	Navarre	Navarra
Estepa	red			Seville	
Estepona	*See* MALAGA			Málaga	Málaga
Ezcaba 'Chacolí'	red	dry	light	Navarre	Navarra
Falces	*clarete* red	dry	high a/c ord., medium a/c	Navarre	Navarra
Falset	*See* TARRAGONA esp. red	sweet	high a/c	Tarragona	Tarragona
Farlete	*See* Aragon			Zaragoza	
Fefiñanes	white	light	fine	Pontevedra	
Felanitx (Majorca)	white red	sweet sweet		Balearics	
Fermoselle	*clarete* dark red	dry dry	fine strong	Zamora	
Fitero	dark red	dry	strong	Navarre	Navarra
Fogoneu	black			Balearics	
'Fondillon'	red	sweet	high a/c	Alicante	Alicante
Fontrubí	*See* PANADES, Upper			Barcelona	Panadés
Fortuna	red	semi-sweet (becoming drier with age)	strong	Murcia	
Frasno, El	*See* CARIÑENA			Zaragoza	Cariñena
Fregenal de la Sierra	*clarete*	dry	medium a/c	Badajoz	
Fuencarral 'Moscatel' 'Pardillo blanco de Tierra de Madrid'	golden golden	sweet sweet		Madrid	
Fuenmayor	*See* RIOJA			Logroño	Rioja (Alta)
Fuente del Maestre	white		ord., medium a/c	Badajoz	
Fuenteovejuna	*See* MONTILLA			Córdoba	Montilla-Moriles

NAME	DESCRIPTION			PROVINCE	DENOMINA- CION DE ORIGEN
Fuenterrobles	*See* UTIEL			Valencia	Utell- Requena
Fuentesaúco	*clarete*	dry	fine	Zamora	
	dark red	dry	strong		
Fuentes de Ebro	*See* Aragon			Zaragoza	
Fuentes del Jiloca	*See* Aragon			Zaragoza	
Gandesa	*See* TARRAGONA			Tarragona	Tarragona
Garganta de la Olla	red	dry	ord.	Cáceres	
Garnacha blanca	white			Barcelona Logroño Tarragona	
Garnacha peluda	black			Tarragona	
Garnacha tinta	black			Alicante Barcelona Gerona Logroño Madrid Navarre Orense Salamanca Tarragona Valencia Valladolid Zamora Zaragoza	
Garrido fino	white			Cádiz	
Gata	red	dry	ord.	Cáceres	
Gaucín	*See* MALAGA			Málaga	Málaga
Getafe	red		ord., high a/c	Madrid	
Graciano	black			Alava Logroño Navarre	
Granada, La	*See* PANADES, Central			Barcelona	Panadés
Gran Canaria (island)	white	dry		Las Palmas (Canary Is.)	
	white	sweet			
Grañen	*See* Aragon			Huesca	
Grao, El	*See* VALENCIA			Valencia	Valencia
Gratallops	*See* PRIORATO			Tarragona	Priorato
Grazalema	white			Cádiz	
Guadalajara 'Pardillo'	golden	sweet		Guadalajara	
Guadalcanal	white		light	Seville	
	clarete	semi-sweet			
	red	sweet			

NAME	DESCRIPTION			PROVINCE	DENOMINA-CION DE ORIGEN
Guadalcazar	*See* MONTILLA			Córdoba	Montilla-Moriles
Guadix	red			Granada	
Guareña	white		ord., medium a/c	Badajoz	
	red	dry			
Guetaria				Guipúzcoa	
'Chacolí'	white	acrid	low a/c		
	and red	acrid	low a/c		
Haro	*See* RIOJA			Logroño	Rioja (Alta)
Hellín	red	semi-sweet	strong	Albacete	
Herradilla	black			Santander	
Hervás	red	dry		Cáceres	
Hierro (island)	white	dry		Santa Cruz	
	white	sweet		de Tenerife (Canary Is.)	
Híjar	*See* Aragon			Teruel	
Hinojos	*See* HUELVA			Huelva	Huelva
Hondón de los Frailes	*See* ALICANTE			Alicante	Alicante
Horcajo de Santiago	*See* MANCHA esp. red wines			Cuenca	
Hoyos	white			Cáceres	
	clarete	dry			
	red	dry	ord.		
HUELVA	white	usu. sweet	strong	Huelva	Huelva
	red	sweet	strong		
Huércanos	*See* RIOJA			Logroño	Rioja (Alta)
Huerta	*See* MANCHA			Toledo	Mancha
Ibi	*See* ALICANTE			Alicante	Alicante
Ibiza (island)	red	sweet		Balearics	
Igualada	white			Barcelona	
Illana	white		ord.	Guadalajara	
	red		ord.		
Inca (Majorca)	red	sweet		Balearics	
Iniesta	*See* MANCHA esp. red		strong	Cuenca	Mancha
Jaén blanco	white			Albacete Badajoz Ciudad Real Cuenca Málaga Toledo	
Jaén doradillo	white (golden)			Málaga	
Jaén tinto	black			Málaga	
Jana, La	red		high a/c	Castellón de la Plana	

NAME	DESCRIPTION			PROVINCE	DENOMINA-CION DE ORIGEN
Jaraiz	red	dry	ord.	Cáceres	
Jarandilla	red	dry	ord.	Cáceres	
Jatiel	*See* Aragon			Teruel	
Játiva	*See* VALENCIA			Valencia	Valencia
	esp. white		light, table		
Jerez de la Frontera	*See* SHERRY			Cádiz	Jerez-Xérès-Sherry
Also 'Pajarete' 'Pajareto' }	golden	sweet	high a/c		
	red		ord.		
JUMILLA	*rosado*		high a/c	Murcia	Jumilla
	red		strong		
Labastida	*See* RIOJA			Alava	Rioja (Alavesa)
	esp. red	semi-sweet	light		
'Lágrima'	*See* MALAGA			Málaga	Málaga
Laguardia	*See* RIOJA			Alava	Rioja (Alavesa)
	esp. red	dry	strong		
Lairén	white			Badajoz Córdoba Málaga	
Lalueza	*See* Aragon			Huesca	
Lanaja	*See* Aragon			Huesca	
Lanzarote (island)	white	dry		Las Palmas (Canary Is.)	
	white	sweet			
Lebeña	red	dry		Santander	
'Tostadillo'	golden	sweet	high a/c		
Leiro	*See* RIBERO			Orense	Ribero
Leza	*See* RIOJA			Alava	Rioja (Alavesa)
Liébana (region)	*rosado*	coarse	low a/c	Santander	
	red	coarse	low a/c		
'Tostadillo'	golden	sweet	high a/c		
Lillo	*See* MANCHA			Toledo	Mancha
Limpias	*clarete*	dry	low a/c	Santander	
Liria	*See* VALENCIA			Valencia	Valencia
	esp. red wines				
Listán	white			Santa Cruz de Tenerife (Canary Is.) Las Palmas (Canary Is.)	
Llacuna, La	*See* PANADES, Upper			Barcelona	Panadés
Llansá	white	sweet		Gerona	
	red	sweet	high a/c		
Lledoner	black			Gerona	
Lloá	*See* PRIORATO			Tarragona	Priorato
Lluchmayor (Majorca)	white	sweet		Balearics	
	red	sweet			
Loarre	*See* Aragon			Huesca	
Logroño	*See* RIOJA			Logroño	Rioja (Alta)
Lopera	white			Jaén	

NAME	DESCRIPTION			PROVINCE	DENOMINA-CION DE ORIGEN
Lucena	*See* MORILES			Córdoba	Montilla-Moriles
Lumbier	red		ord., low a/c	Navarre	Navarra
Lumpiaque	*See* Aragon			Zaragoza	
Macabeo	white			Barcelona Tarragona	
Macharnudo	*See* SHERRY esp. 'Amontillado'			Cádiz	Jerez-Xérès-Sherry
Madridanos	*clarete* dark red	dry dry	fine strong	Zamora	
Madridejos	*See* MANCHA			Toledo	Mancha
Madrigueras	*clarete*		high a/c	Albacete	
Madroñales	*See* SHERRY esp. 'Moscatel'			Cádiz	Jerez-Xérès-Sherry
Maella	*See* Aragon			Zaragoza	
Mahón (Minorca)	red	sweet		Balearics	
MALAGA				Málaga	Málaga
'Blanco seco'	pale	dry			
'Semidulce'	pale	semi-sweet			
'Moscatel'	golden	sweet			
'Pedro Xim-énez'	golden	sweet			
'Rome'	golden	sweet			
'Pajarete'	golden	sweet			
'Dulce blanco dorado'	dark golden	sweet			
'Dulce oscuro'	dark	sweet			
'Lágrima'	dark	very sweet			
'Tintillo'	dark red	sweet			
Mallén	*See* Aragon			Zaragoza	
Malvasía ('Malvasía', Malmsey)	white			Alava Alicante Barcelona Las Palmas (Canary Is.) Logroño Santa Cruz de Tenerife (Canary Is.) Tarragona Valencia Valladolid Zamora	
MANCHA, La	white rosado *clarete* dry esp. 'Tinto de Valdepeñas'		ord., usu. strong ord., usu. strong strong	Albacete Ciudad Real Cuenca Toledo	Mancha

NAME	DESCRIPTION			PROVINCE	DENOMINA-CION DE ORIGEN
Mancha La white	red white	bitter- sweet	ord., usu. strong		
Mañeru	red	dry	low a/c	Navarre	Navarra
Manto negro	black			Majorca	
Mantuo fino	white			Cádiz	
Mantuo pila	white			Cádiz	
Manzanares	*See* MANCHA			Ciudad Real	Mancha
'Manzanilla'	*See* SHERRY			Cádiz	Jerez-Xérès-Sherry
Manzanilla	*See* HUELVA			Huelva	Huelva
Marsá	*See* TARRAGONA esp. red	sweet	high a/c	Tarragona	Tarragona
Martino	white			Santander	
Martorell	white	dry	low a/c	Barcelona	
Martos	white *clarete* red			Jaén	
Masnou	*See* ALELLA			Barcelona	Alella
Masquefa	*See* PANADES, Upper			Barcelona	Panadés
Mazuelo	black			Alava Logroño	
Medina del Campo	white *clarete* red	dry dry dry	medium a/c strong ord.	Valladolid	
Medina Sidonia	white	dry		Cádiz	
Mediona	*See* PANADES, Upper			Barcelona	Panadés
Meira 'Albariño'	white		fine	Pontevedra	
Membrilla	*See* MANCHA			Ciudad Real	Mancha
Mencía	black			León Orense	
Mendigorría	red	dry	low a/c	Navarre	Navarra
Méntrida	*See* MANCHA			Toledo	Mancha
Mérida	white		ord., medium a/c	Badajoz	
Merseguera	white			Valencia	
Mesas, Las	*See* MANCHA			Cuenca	Mancha
Miajadas	white *clarete*		ord., medium a/c	Cáceres	
Minglanilla	*See* MANCHA esp. red		strong	Cuenca	Mancha
Miraflores	*See* SHERRY esp. 'Manzanilla'			Cádiz	Jerez-Xérès-Sherry
Miranda	dark red	dry		Salamanca	
Moguer	*See* HUELVA			Huelva	Huelva
Moja (Barcelona)	*See* PANADES			Barcelona	Panadés
Molvizar	white	sweet		Granada	
Mombeltrán	red		ord.	Avila	

NAME	DESCRIPTION			PROVINCE	DENOMINA-CION DE ORIGEN
Monforte de Lemos	red	acrid	thick	Lugo	
Mongat	*See* ALELLA			Barcelona	Alella
Monjos (Barcelona)	*See* PANADES			Barcelona	Panadés
Monóvar	*See* ALICANTE			Alicante	Alicante
Montánchez	white			Cáceres	
	clarete	dry			
	red	dry			
Montblanch	*See* Conca de Barbará			Tarragona	
Montbrió esp.	*See* TARRAGONA			Tarragona	Tarragona
'Moscatel'	white	sweet			
Monteagudo	red	dry	medium to high a/c	Navarre	Navarra
Montehermoso	*clarete*	dry		Cáceres	
Monterrey	white	dry	light	Orense	
	red	dry			
Monterrubio de la Serena	white	sweet	high a/c	Badajoz	
Montijo	white		ord., medium a/c	Badajoz	
	red				
MONTILLA	(Unfortified wines)			Córdoba	Montilla-Moriles
'Fino'	pale	dry			
'Fino viejo' ('Amontillado')	pale	dry			
'Oloroso'	golden	usu. sweet strong-scented			
'Oloroso viejo'	golden	usu. sweet strong-scented			
'Pedro Ximénez'	golden	very sweet			
Montmell	*See* PANADES, Central			Tarragona	Panadés
Montroig	*See* TARRAGONA			Tarragona	Tarragona
Mora	*See* MANCHA			Toledo	Mancha
Moraleja del Vino	*clarete*	dry	fine	Zamora	
	dark red	dry	strong		
Morastrell	black			Alicante Barcelona Murcia Tarragona Valencia Zaragoza	
Morata del Jalón	*See* Aragon			Zaragoza	
Moratalla	red	semi-sweet strong (becoming drier with age)		Murcia	
Morera, La	*See* PRIORATO			Tarragona	Priorato
MORILES	(Unfortified wines) Very similar to MONTILLA wines, and blended with them			Córdoba	Montilla-Moriles

NAME	DESCRIPTION			PROVINCE	DENOMINA-CION DE ORIGEN
'Moscatel'	*See* SHERRY and others, e.g. Sitges			Cádiz	Jerez-Xérès-Sherry
Moscatel	white			Alicante Barcelona Cádiz Córdoba Málaga Tarragona Valencia Valladolid Zamora	
Mota del Cuervo	*See* MANCHA			Cuenca	Mancha
Motilla del Palancar	*See* MANCHA esp. red		strong	Cuenca	Mancha
Mula	red (becoming drier with age)	semi-sweet	strong	Murcia	
Murillo de Río Leza	*See* RIOJA esp. red	dry	strong	Logroño	Rioja (Baja)
Nájera	*See* RIOJA			Logroño	Rioja (Alta)
Nava del Rey	white	dry	medium a/c	Valladolid	
	clarete	dry	light		
	red	dry	ord.		
Navalcarnero	red		ord., very high a/c	Madrid	
NAVARRE	white	dry	light	Navarre	Navarra
	golden	sweet	high a/c		
	clarete	dry	low a/c		
	clarete	dry	high a/c		
	red	dry	low a/c		
	red	light	medium a/c		
	dark red	dry	strong		
	white (small quantities)		sparkling		
Navarrete	*See* RIOJA esp. white	semi-sweet	light	Logroño	Rioja (Alta)
Negra de Almendralejo	black			Badajoz	
Negrín	black			Oviedo	
Nerja	*See* MALAGA			Málaga	Málaga
Niebla	*See* HUELVA			Huelva	Huelva
Noblejas	*See* MANCHA			Toledo	Mancha
Nules	red		high a/c	Castellón de la Plana	
Ocaña	*See* MANCHA			Toledo	Mancha
Olesa de Bonesválls	*See* PANADES, Central			Barcelona	Panadés
Olite	red		ord., medium a/c	Navarre	Navarra

NAME	DESCRIPTION			PROVINCE	DENOMINA-CION DE ORIGEN
Olivares	usu. white	sweet	strong	Seville	
Olivares de Duero	white red	dry dry	strong ord.	Valladolid	
Ollauri	*See* RIOJA			Logroño	Rioja (Alta)
Olmos, Los	*See* Aragon			Teruel	
'Oloroso'	*See* SHERRY			Cádiz	Jerez-Xérès-Sherry
Olvera	white	dry		Cádiz	
Onteniente	*See* VALENCIA esp. red wines			Valencia	Valencia
Orense	*See* RIBERO also white		sparkling	Orense	Ribero
Orgaz	*See* MANCHA			Toledo	Mancha
Orihuela de Segura	*See* ALICANTE esp. red	sweet		Alicante	Alicante
Oropesa	red		high a/c	Castellón de la Plana	
Orotava, La	white esp. 'Malvasía'	sweet	high a/c	Santa Cruz de Tenerife (Canary Is.)	
Pachs del Panadés	*See* PANADES			Barcelona	Panadés
'Pajarete'	golden	sweet	high a/c	Cádiz Málaga	
'Pajareto'	golden-brown	sweet	high a/c	Cádiz Seville	
'Palma'	*See* SHERRY			Cádiz	Jerez-Xérès-Sherry
Palma, La (island)	white white esp. 'Moscatel'	dry sweet		Santa Cruz de Tenerife (Canary Is.)	
Palma del Condado, La	*See* HUELVA			Huelva	Huelva
Palma del Río	*See* MONTILLA			Córdoba	Montilla-Moriles
'Palo cortado'	*See* SHERRY			Cádiz	Jerez-Xérès-Sherry
Palomino	white			Málaga Valladolid Zamora	
Palomino de Jerez	white			Cádiz	
Palos de la Frontera	*See* HUELVA			Huelva	Huelva
Pamplona	white red	dry dry	light light	Navarre	Navarra
PANADES, Upper	white white	dry semi-dry	low a/c low a/c	Barcelona Tarragona	Panadés

NAME	DESCRIPTION			PROVINCE	DENOMINA-CION DE ORIGEN
PANADES,					
Central	white	dry	medium a/c		
	white	semi-dry	medium a/c		
	white		sparkling		
Lower	white	semi-dry	usu. high a/c		
	rosado	dry	usu. high a/c		
	red	dry	usu. high a/c		
	red	semi-dry	usu. high a/c		
	red	sweet	high a/c		
Paniza	*See* CARIÑENA			Zaragoza	Cariñena
	esp. red	sweet			
Paracuellos de Jiloca	*See* Aragon			Zaragoza	
Pardillo	white			Cuenca Guadalajara Madrid	
Parduca	black			Santander	
Paredes de Nava	white	dry		Palencia	
Pastrana	red		ord.	Guadalajara	
Peares, Los	red	dry		Lugo	
Pedralba	*See* VALENCIA			Valencia	Valencia
Pedrola	*See* Aragon			Zaragoza	
Pedroñeras, Las	*See* MANCHA esp. white		ord., medium a/c	Cuenca	Mancha
'Pedro Ximénez'	*See* SHERRY			Cádiz	Jerez-Xérès-Sherry
Pedro Ximénez, P.X., Pedro Ximén, Perojiménez, or Perojimén	white			Barcelona Cádiz Córdoba Las Palmas (Canary Is.) Málaga Santa Cruz de Tenerife (Canary Is.) Seville Tarragona	
Pelayos	white	dry		Salamanca	
Peleagonzalo	*clarete*	dry	fine	Zamora	
	dark red	dry	strong		
Peñafiel	white	dry	ord.	Valladolid	
	clarete	dry	light		
	red	dry	ord.		
Peñíscola	red		high a/c	Castellón de la Plana	
Peralta	golden	sweet	high a/c	Navarre	Navarra
Perelada	white	dry	light	Gerona	
	rosado	dry	light		
Perelada	red		ord.		
	red	sweet	high a/c		
	white	dry	sparkling		

NAME	DESCRIPTION			PROVINCE	DENOMINA-CION DE ORIGEN
Pereña	red	dry		Salamanca	
Perruno fino	white			Cádiz	
Picapoll	white			Barcelona	
				Tarragona	
	black			Tarragona	
Piera	*rosado*		medium a/c	Barcelona	
	red		medium a/c		
Pierola	*rosado*		medium a/c	Barcelona	
	red		medium a/c		
Pilas	usu. white	sweet	strong	Seville	
Pinell de Bray	white	sweet	medium a/c	Tarragona	
	rosado	sweet	medium a/c		
	red	sweet	medium a/c		
Pinoso	*See* ALICANTE			Alicante	Alicante
Pinto	red		ord., high a/c	Madrid	
Pira	*See* Conca de Barbará			Tarragona	
Pitillas	*clarete*	dry	high a/c	Navarre	Navarra
	red		ord., medium a/c		
Planta de Pedralba	white			Valencia	
Planta Nova	white			Valencia	
Plasencia	white			Cáceres	
	clarete	dry			
Poboleda	*See* PRIORATO			Tarragona	Priorato
esp. 'Malvasía'	white	sweet	high a/c		
Pollensa (Majorca)	red	sweet		Balearics	
'Malvasía'	white	sweet	high a/c		
Ponsal	white			Balearics	
				Tarragona	
Pontóns	*See* PANADES, Upper			Barcelona	Panadés
Ponzano	*See* Aragon			Huesca	
Porrera	*See* PRIORATO			Tarragona	Priorato
Posadas	*See* MONTILLA			Córdoba	Montilla-Moriles
Pozáldez	white	dry	medium a/c	Valladolid	
	clarete	dry	light		
	red	dry	ord.		
Priego de Córdoba	*See* MORILES			Córdoba	Montilla-Moriles
Prieto Picudo	black			León Salamanca Valladolid Zamora	
PRIORATO	white	dry	high a/c	Tarragona	Priorato
	white	sweet	high a/c		
	rosado	dry	high a/c		
	rosado	sweet	high a/c		
	red	dry	high a/c		
	red	sweet	high a/c		

Plate 15. The Sherry grape: the Palomino (*see* Chapter 2)

Percy Hennell

NAME	DESCRIPTION			PROVINCE	DENOMINA-CION DE ORIGEN
'Rancio'	golden	dry and sweet	high a/c		
'Malvasía'	white	sweet	high a/c		
'Pedro Ximénez'	golden	sweet	high a/c		
Provencio, El	*See* MANCHA			Cuenca	Mancha
Puebla, La (Majorca)	white red	sweet sweet		Balearics	
Puebla de Almoradiel, La	*See* MANCHA			Toledo	Mancha
Puebla de Híjar, La	*See* Aragon			Teruel	
Puebla del Duc	*See* VALENCIA esp. white	light	table	Valencia	Valencia
Puente Canedos	*See* RIBERO			Orense	Ribero
Puente Genil	*See* MORILES			Córdoba	Montilla-Moriles
Puente la Reina	white red	dry	low a/c	Navarre	Navarra
Puerto de Santa María	*See* SHERRY			Cádiz	Jerez-Xérès-Sherry
Puerto Real	white	dry		Cádiz	
Purchena	red		table	Almería	
Quel	*See* RIOJA esp. red	dry	strong	Logroño	Rioja (Baja)
Quero	*See* MANCHA			Toledo	Mancha
Quintanar de la Orden	*See* MANCHA			Toledo	Mancha
Quintanar del Rey	*See* MANCHA esp. red		strong	Cuenca	Mancha
Quiroga	red	acrid	thick	Lugo	
Ramallosa	red	acrid	thick	Pontevedra	
Rambla, La	*See* MONTILLA			Córdoba	Montilla-Moriles
'Raya'	*See* SHERRY			Cádiz	Jerez Xérès-Sherry
Real de Montroy	*See* CHESTE			Valencia	Cheste
Regadio, El	*See* Aragon			Teruel	
Renera 'Aloque'	red		ord.	Guadalajara	
REQUENA	red dark red	light	table rich	Valencia	Utiel-Requena
Reus	*See* TARRAGONA			Tarragona	Tarragona
Ribadavia	*See* RIBERO			Orense	Ribero
Ribadeneira	red	acrid	thick	Lugo	

K

NAME	DESCRIPTION			PROVINCE	DENOMINA-CION DE ORIGEN
RIBERO	white	dry	fine	Orense	Ribero
(or Ribeiro)	red	semi-dry	light		
'Tostado'	golden	sweet	high a/c		
'Tostadillo'	golden	sweet	high a/c		
Ricardell	red	sweet	high a/c	Gerona	
Ricla	*See* Aragon			Zaragoza	
Rincón	*See* RIOJA			Logroño	Rioja (Baja)
de Soto	esp. red	dry	strong		
RIOJA	white	dry		Alava	Rioja
	white	semi-dry		Burgos	
	white	semi-sweet		Logroño	
	white	sweet		Navarre	
	rosado	dry	light		
	clarete	dry	light		
	red	dry			
	red	semi-dry			
	white		sparkling		
Robledillo	white	dry		Cáceres	
de Gata					
Robres	*See* Aragon			Huesca	
Rociana del	*See* HUELVA			Huelva	Huelva
Condado					
Roda, La	*See* MANCHA			Albacete	Mancha
	esp. red		strong		
Roda de Bara	*See* PANADES, Lower			Tarragona	Panadés
Rodillana	white	dry	medium a/c	Valladolid	
	clarete	dry	light		
	red	dry	ord.		
Rodriguillo, El	*See* ALICANTE			Alicante	Alicante
Romana, La	*See* ALICANTE			Alicante	Alicante
Rome	white			Málaga	
Rosal	red	acrid	thick	Pontevedra	
Rota	*See* SHERRY			Cádiz	Jerez-Xérès-Sherry
	esp. 'Moscatel'				
'Rota Tent'	dark red	bitter	fortified	Cádiz	
(= 'Tintilla')					
Rourell	*See* TARRAGONA			Tarragona	Tarragona
Rúa de	*See* VALDEORRAS			Orense	Valdeorras
Valdeorras					
Rubí	white	dry	low a/c	Barcelona	
Rueda	white	dry	medium a/c	Valladolid	
	clarete	dry	light		
	red	dry	ord.		
Rute	*See* MORILES			Córdoba	Montilla-Moriles
Sacedón	red		ord.	Guadalajara	
Sagra, La	*See* MANCHA			Toledo	Mancha
Sagunto	*See* VALENCIA			Valencia	Valencia
	esp. red	sweet	rich		
Sahagún	red	dry, acrid		León	
Salamanca	red	dry		Salamanca	

NAME	DESCRIPTION			PROVINCE	DENOMINA-CION DE ORIGEN
Salas	*See* Aragon			Huesca	
Salinas	*See* ALICANTE			Alicante	Alicante
Salsadella	red		high a/c	Castellón de la Plana	
Salvatierra de los Barros	dark red			Badajoz	
Salvatierra de Miño	red	acrid	thick	Pontevedra	
Samper de Calanda	*See* Aragon			Teruel	
San Adrián	*See* RIOJA esp. red		ord., medium a/c	Navarre	Rioja (Baja)
San Asensio	*See* RIOJA			Logroño	Rioja (Alta)
San Baudilio de Llobregat	white *rosado* red	semi-sweet		Barcelona	
San Clemente	*See* MANCHA esp. red wines			Cuenca	Mancha
San Cugat del Vallés	white	dry	low a/c	Barcelona	
Sangüesa	red		ord., low a/c	Navarre	Navarra
San Juan del Puerto	*See* HUELVA			Huelva	Huelva
San Lorenzo de Hortons	*See* PANADES, Upper			Barcelona	Panadés
San Lorenzo Savall	white	dry	low a/c	Barcelona	
Sanlúcar de Barrameda Also 'Jaloque'	*See* SHERRY esp. 'Manzanilla' white			Cádiz	Jerez-Xérès-Sherry
Sanlúcar la Mayor	usu. white	sweet	strong	Seville	
San Martín de Valdeiglesias	white red		ord. ord., high a/c	Madrid	
San Mateo	red	semi-sweet	high a/c	Castellón de la Plana	
San Roque	white	dry		Cádiz	
San Sadurní de Noya	*See* PANADES, Central esp. sparkling			Barcelona	Panadés
Santa Cruz de la Zarza	*See* MANCHA			Toledo	Mancha
Santañy (Majorca)	white red	sweet sweet		Balearics	
Santas Creus	*See* PANADES, Central			Tarragona	Panadés
San Vicente de la Sonsierra	*See* RIOJA esp. red	semi-sweet	light	Logroño	Rioja (Alta)
Sanzoles	*clarete* dark red	dry dry	fine strong	Zamora	
Sariñena	*See* Aragon			Huesca	

NAME	DESCRIPTION			PROVINCE	DENOMINA-CION DE ORIGEN
Sástago	*See* Aragon			Zaragoza	
Sax	*See* ALICANTE			Alicante	Alicante
Sayalonga	*See* MALAGA			Málaga	Málaga
Seca, La	white	dry	medium a/c	Valladolid	
	clarete	dry	light		
	red	dry	ord.		
Secuita, La	*See* TARRAGONA			Tarragona	Tarragona
	esp. white	sweet			
Segorbe	red		high a/c	Castellón de la Plana	
Selva, La	*See* TARRAGONA			Tarragona	Tarragona
	esp. white	sweet			
SHERRY, Jerez, or Xérès	(Fortified wines)			Cádiz	Jerez-Xérès-Sherry
'Fino'	pale	dry			
'Palma'	pale	dry			
'Amontillado'	pale	dry			
'Manzanilla'	golden	dry	light		
'Moscatel'	golden	sweet			
'Palo cortado'	dark		strong		
'Oloroso'	usu. dark	sweet	strong		
'Raya'	dark		strong		
'Pedro Ximénez'	dark	very sweet			
Simancas	white	dry	medium a/c	Valladolid	
	clarete	dry	strong		
	red	dry	ord.		
Sineu (Majorca)	white	sweet		Balearics	
	red	sweet			
Sisante	*See* MANCHA			Cuenca	Mancha
	esp. red		strong		
Sitges	*See* PANADES, Lower			Barcelona	Panadés
Also					
'Malvasía'	white	sweet			
'Moscatel'	white	sweet			
Socuéllamos	*See* MANCHA			Ciudad Real	Mancha
Solana, La	*See* MANCHA			Ciudad Real	Mancha
Solana de los Barros	white		ord., medium a/c	Badajoz	
	red				
Subirats	*See* PANADES, Central			Barcelona	Panadés
Sumoll	black			Barcelona	
Tafalla	red	dry	medium to high a/c	Navarre	Navarra
Talavera	*See* MANCHA			Toledo	Mancha
Tarancón	*See* MANCHA			Cuenca	Mancha
Tarazona de Aragón	*See* Aragon			Zaragoza	

NAME	DESCRIPTION			PROVINCE	DENOMINA-CION DE ORIGEN
TARRAGONA					
	white	dry	medium a/c	Tarragona	Tarragona
	white	semi-dry	medium a/c		
	white	semi-sweet	medium a/c		
	white	sweet	high a/c		
	white	very sweet	fortified		
	rosado	semi-sweet	high a/c		
	red	dry	high a/c		
	red	sweet	high a/c		
	white		sparkling		
	(in small quantities)				
Tarrasa	white	dry	low a/c	Barcelona	
Tehigo	dark red	bitter	fortified	Cádiz	Jerez-Xérès-
'Tintilla'					Sherry
Teide	white	sweet		Santa Cruz	
				de Tenerife	
				(Canary Is.)	
Tempranillo	black			Alava	
				Alella	
				Orense	
				Pontevedra	
				Valladolid	
				Zamora	
Tenerife	white		ord.	Santa Cruz de	
(island)				Tenerife	
'Malvasía'	golden	sweet	high a/c	(Canary Is.)	
'Tent'	*See* 'Rota Tent'				
Tercios, Los	*See* SHERRY			Cádiz	Jerez-Xérès-
	esp. 'Fino'				Sherry
Terrateig	*See* VALENCIA			Valencia	Valencia
	esp. white	light	table		
Teyá	*See* ALELLA			Barcelona	Alella
Tiana	*See* ALELLA			Barcelona	Alella
Tiebas	*clarete*	dry	high a/c	Navarre	Navarra
	red	light	medium a/c		
Tinta	black			Cuenca	
Tinta de Toro	black			Zamora	
'Tintilla'	*See* 'Rota Tent'				
Tintorera	black			Alicante	
				Ciudad Real	
				Toledo	
Tirgo	*See* RIOJA			Logroño	Rioja (Alta)
Tivisa	*See* TARRAGONA			Tarragona	Tarragona
Tobarra	red	semi-sweet	strong	Albacete	
Toboso, El	*See* MANCHA			Toledo	Mancha
Tomelloso	*See* MANCHA			Ciudad Real	Mancha
Tordesillas	white	dry	ord.	Valladolid	
	clarete	dry	light		
	red	dry	ord.		
Toro	*clarete*	dry	fine	Zamora	
	dark red	dry	strong		
Torrebreba	*See* SHERRY			Cádiz	Jerez-Xérès-
	esp. 'Manzanilla'				Sherry

NAME	DESCRIPTION			PROVINCE	DENOMINA-CION DE ORIGEN
Torre de Don Miguel	red	dry	ord.	Cáceres	
Torre del Campo	*clarete* red			Jaén	
Torredembarra	*See* TARRAGONA			Tarragona	Tarragona
Torredon-jimeno	white			Jaén	
Torrelaguna	red	acrid	ord.	Madrid	
Torremegía	white		ord., medium a/c	Badajoz	
Torrente	*See* VALENCIA esp. dark red		rich	Valencia	Valencia
Torreperojil	*clarete* red			Jaén	
Torrijos	*See* MANCHA			Toledo	Mancha
Torroja	*See* PRIORATO			Tarragona	Priorato
Torrontés	white			Orense	
Torrox	*See* MALAGA			Málaga	Málaga
'Tostadillo'	golden	sweet	high a/c	Orense Santander	
'Tostado'	dark golden	sweet	high a/c	Orense	
Totana	red (becoming drier with age)	semi-sweet	strong	Murcia	
Traiguera	red	semi-sweet	high a/c	Castellón de la Plana	
Trebujena	*See* SHERRY			Cádiz	Jerez-Xérès-Sherry
Treixadura	white			Orense	
Tricio	*See* RIOJA			Logroño	Rioja (Alta)
Trigueros	*See* HUELVA			Huelva	Huelva
Trujillo	*clarete* red	dry dry	strong	Cáceres	
Tudela	red	dry	medium to high a/c	Navarre	Navarra
Tudelilla	*See* RIOJA			Logroño	Rioja (Baja)
Turis	*See* CHESTE esp. white white	light sweet	ord. high a/c	Valencia	Cheste
Tuy	red	acrid	thick	Pontevedra	
Ubeda	red			Jaén	
Ubrique	white			Cádiz	
Ullastrell	white	dry	low a/c	Barcelona	
Umbrete	usu. white	sweet	strong	Seville	
Urrera de Gaeno	*See* Aragon			Teruel	
Uruñuela	*See* RIOJA			Logroño	Rioja (Alta)
UTIEL	red	light	table, low a/c	Valencia	Utiel-Requena

NAME	DESCRIPTION			PROVINCE	DENOMINA- CION DE ORIGEN
Valdefinjas	*clarete*	dry	fine	Zamora	
	dark red	dry	strong		
Valdemoro	red		ord., high a/c	Madrid	
VALDEOR- RAS	white	dry	low a/c	Orense	
	red	dry	low a/c		
'Tostado'	dark golden	sweet	high a/c		
Valdepeñas	*See* MANCHA			Ciudad Real	Mancha
'Valdepeñas tinto'	*clarete*	dry	strong	Ciudad Real	Mancha
Valderrobres	*See* Aragon			Teruel	
VALENCIA	white	light	table	Valencia	Valencia
	white	sweet	high a/c		
	rosado	light	table		
	red	light	table		
	red	sweet	rich		
Valladolid	red	dry	ord.	Valladolid	
Valleta	red	sweet	high a/c	Gerona	
Valls	*See* TARRAGONA			Tarragona	Tarragona
	esp. white	sweet			
Valmojado	*See* MANCHA			Toledo	Mancha
Valoría la Buena	red	dry	ord.	Valladolid	
Vega, La (district)	red			Granada	
Vega Sicilia	red	semi-sweet	table	Valladolid	
Vélez Benaudalla	red			Granada	
Vélez-Málaga	*See* MALAGA			Málaga	Málaga
Vendrell	*See* PANADES, Lower			Tarragona	Panadés
Venialbo	*clarete*	dry	fine	Zamora	
	dark red	dry	strong		
Venta del Moro	*See* UTIEL, REQUENA			Valencia	Utiel- Requena
Verdejo blanco	white			Valladolid	
Verdejo tinto	black			León Salamanca Valladolid Zamora	
Verín	red	dry	light	Orense	
Vilajuïga	white	sweet	high a/c	Gerona	
	red	sweet	high a/c		
	red		ord.		
Vilarrodona	*See* TARRAGONA			Tarragona	Tarragona
Vilaseca de Solcina	*See* TARRAGONA esp. white	sweet		Tarragona	Tarragona
Vilellas, Las	*See* PRIORATO			Tarragona	Priorato
Villacarrillo	red			Jaén	
Villa de Don Fadrique	*See* MANCHA			Toledo	Mancha
Villaescusa	*clarete*	dry	fine	Zamora	
	dark red	dry	strong		
Villafeliche	*See* Aragon			Zaragoza	

NAME	DESCRIPTION			PROVINCE	DENOMINA-CION DE ORIGEN
Villafranca	red	dry	acrid	León	
Villafranca	*See* Peralta			Navarre	Navarra
Villafranca del Bierzo	*See* VALDEORRAS			León	Valdeorras
Villafranca de los Barros	white		ord., medium a/c	Badajoz	
Villafranca del Panadés	*See* PANADES, Central			Barcelona	Panadés
Villagonzalo	white		ord., medium a/c	Badajoz	
Villalazán	*clarete*	dry	fine	Zamora	
	dark red	dry	strong		
Villalba del Alcor	*See* HUELVA			Huelva	Huelva
Villalpando	*clarete*	dry	fine	Zamora	
	dark red	dry	strong		
Villalpardo	*See* MANCHA esp. red		strong	Cuenca	Mancha
Villamañán	red	dry	acrid	León	
Villamartín	white			Cádiz	
Villamayor	red	dry	light	Salamanca	
Villamayor de Santiago	*See* MANCHA esp. red wines			Cuenca	Mancha
Villamayor 'Moscatel'	golden	sweet		Zaragoza	
Villanueva	*See* PANADES, Lower			Barcelona	Panadés
Villanueva de la Jara	*See* MANCHA esp. red		strong	Cuenca	Mancha
Villanueva de la Serena	white		ord., medium a/c	Badajoz	
Villarrasa	*See* HUELVA			Huelva	Huelva
Villar del Arzobispo	*See* VALENCIA esp. white	light	table	Valencia	Valencia
Villarino	red	dry	ord.	Salamanca	
Villarobledo	*See* MANCHA esp. red		strong	Albacete	Mancha
Villaroya de la Sierra	*See* Aragon			Zaragoza	
Villarreal	red		high a/c	Castellón de la Plana	
Villaviciosa de Córdoba	*See* MONTILLA			Córdoba	Montilla-Moriles
Villena	*See* ALICANTE			Alicante	Alicante
Vinaroz	red		high a/c	Castellón de la Plana	
Vinaté	white			Balearics	
Vinebre	*See* TARRAGONA esp. red	sweet	high a/c	Tarragona	Tarragona
Viura	white			Logroño	
Xarello	white			Barcelona	

NAME	DESCRIPTION			PROVINCE	DENOMINA-CION DE ORIGEN
Yecla	*See* JUMILLA			Murcia	Jumilla
Yepes	*See* MANCHA			Toledo	Mancha
Yesa	red		ord., low a/c	Navarre	Navarra
Yeste	red	semi-sweet	strong	Albacete	
Zafra	white			Badajoz	
Zamora	*clarete*	dry	fine	Zamora	
	dark red	dry	strong		
Záncara	*See* MANCHA			Ciudad Real	Mancha

AUTHORIZED EXPORTERS

Under the *Denominaciones de Origen*

JEREZ-XÉRÈS-SHERRY

In Jerez de la Frontera

Hros de A. Abarzuza
Barón de Algar y Cía, S.A.
Manuel de Argüeso, S.A.
B. Benítez Mateos
Bertola, S.A.
Hijos de A. Blázquez
J. Bustamante, S.L.
Miguel Cala
Manuel de la Calle Jiménez
Chaves y González
Eduardo Delage
Celestino Diaz Morales
Jaime F. Diestro
Diez Hermanos
Pedro Domecq, S.A.
F. Espinosa de los Monteros
Manuel Fernández y Cía, S.L.
Fernando García Delgado Sº
Diego García Pérez y Victor
Garvey, S.A.
M. Gil Galan
M. Gil Luque
González Byass y Cía
Alejandro Gordon
Manuel Guerrero y Cía
S. Guerrero Benítez Sº
Onofre Lorente
Emilio Lustau, S.A.
Mackenzie y Cía
Marqués del Mérito, S.A.
Emilio Martín Hidalgo
José Martínez, S.L.
M. Misa, S.A.
Antonio Muñoz Muñoz

Diego Narvaez Pozo
Rafael O'Neale
Rafael Ortega Palencia
Luis Paez Lobato
Palomino & Vergara, S.A.
A. Parra Guerrero
J. Pemartin y Cía, S.A.
Cayetano del Pino y Cía, S.L.
Hros Marqués del Real Tesoro, S.A.
M. A. de la Riva, S.A.
Tomás Rivero y Hnos, S.L.
Sánchez Romate Hnos
J. Ruiz y Cia
Zoilo Ruiz-Mateos, S.A.
Felix Ruiz y Ruiz, S.L.
José Sánchez Mesa
Sandeman Hnos
José de Soto, S.A.
A. R. Valdespino, S.A.
Javier Vergara Gordon
Williams & Humbert Ltd
Wisdom & Warter Ltd

In Puerto de Santa María

Luis Caballero, S.A.
F. del Castillo Baquero
Cuvillo y Cía
Duff Gordon & Co.
González y Cía
F. Javier Jiménez
Hijos de Jiménez Varela
José L. González Obregón
Osborne y Cía, S.A.
Portalto, S.A.

A. y A. Sancho, S.A.
C. y J. de Terry, S.L.
Fernando A. de Terry, S.A.
Ximénez y Cía

In Sanlúcar de Barramenda

Hros de Argüeso, S.A.
Manuel de Argüeso, S.A.
Antonio Barbadillo, S.A.
Hros de M. Barón, S.A.
Vda de E. Bozzano
Hijos de J. Delgado Zuleta
Florido Hermanos
M. García Monge, S.A.
F. García de Velasco

Enrique Gutierrez Renero
Infantes Orleans-Borbon, S.A.E.
Carlos Otaolaurruchi, S.A.
Hijos de A. Pérez Megia, S.R.C.
Hijos de Rainera Pérez Marín
Rafael Reig y Cía
B. Rodríguez La-Cave, S.A.
Pedro Romero, S.A.
Hros de M. Sánchez Ayala
Vinícola Hidalgo, S.A.

In Cádiz

Miguel M. Gómez, S.A.
Lacave y Cía, S.A.

MONTILLA Y MORILES

Alvear, S.A., Montilla
Aragón y Cía, S.A., Lucena
Baena, S.A., Montilla
Pérez Barquero, S.A., Montilla
Carbonell y Cía, de Córdoba, S.A.,
  Córdoba
J. Cobos, S.A., Montilla

Rafael Cruz Conde, S.A., Montilla
Moreno, S.A., Córdoba
Montialbero, S.A., Montilla
Luís Ortiz-Ruiz y Ortiz, Montilla
Julián Ramírez Pino 'Bodegas Montu-
  lia', Montilla
Miguel Velasco Chacón, S.A., Montilla

RIOJA

Bodegas Berberana, S.A., Ollauri
Bodegas Bilbainas, S.A., Haro
Bodegas Entrena, S.A., Navarrete
Bodegas Franco Españolas, Logroño
Bodegas Gómez Cruzado, S.A., Haro
R. López de Heredia, Viña Tondonia,
  S.A., Haro
Bodegas Lagunilla, S.A., Cenicero
Martínez Lacuesta Hermanos, Ltda,
  Haro
Bodegas Montecillo, S.A., Fuenmayor
Bodegas Muerza, S.A., San Adrián
Bodegas Marqués de Murrieta, Logroño
Bodegas Palacio, S.A., Laguardia
Federico Paternina, S.A., Haro

Bodegas Ramón Bilbao, Haro
La Rioja Alta, S.A., Haro
Bodegas Riojanas, S.A., Cenicero
Bodegas Rioja Santiago, S.A., Haro
Vinos de los Herederos del Marqués de
  Riscal, S.A., Elciego
Bodegas del Romeral, Félix Azpilicueta
  Martínez, S.A., Fuenmayor
Savin, S.A., Aldeanueva de Ebro
Carlos Serres, Hijo, Haro
Andrés de la Torre y Torres, Alfaro
Bodegas Las Veras, Cruz García
  Lafuente, S.A., Fuenmayor
Compañía Vinícola del Norte de
  España, Haro

MANCHA

Bodegas Alfredo, Valdepeñas
Bodegas Bilbainas, S.A., Valdepeñas
Cruzares, S.A., Valdepeñas
Carmelo Madrid, S.A., Valdepeñas

Luis Megía Cruz, Valdepeñas
Gerardo Sánchez Gómez, Bodegas
   Morenito, Valdepeñas
Abel Tarancón Rodero, Valdepeñas

MALAGA

Bodegas La Abadía
Bodegas La Aurora
Hijos de Antonio Barceló, S.A.
Luis Barceló, S.A.
Ricardo Barceló
E. Crooke
Dalmau Hermanos y Cía Sucesores
Flores Hermanos, S.A.
José Mª Flores e Hijos
José Garijo Ruiz
J. González Castro
Hacienda Vinícola Fiammuva
Hijos de Manuel A. Heredia
Guillermo Klein
Bodegas Krauel
Larios, S.A.
Federico Leal

López Hermanos, S.A.
Hijo de Quirico López
Bodegas Malagueñas
Compañía Mata, S.A.
José Mata
Juan Mory y Cía
Hijo de Salvador Pérez Marín
Pérez Texeira, S.A.
C. Rein y S.
Guillermo Rein Segura
T. Rein y Cía
Barón del Rivero
Scholtz Hermanos, S.A.
Souvirón Hermanos, S.A.
La Vinícola de Andalucía, S.A.
Bodegas de La Victoria
Vicusol, S.A.

ALICANTE

Francisco Agulló y Cía, Elche
José de Barrio Sucesor, Alicante
Bodega Cooperativa, Monóvar
Antonio Tomás Conca, Villena
Exportadora de Vinos, S.A., Monóvar
Sebastián Fernández González, Alicante

Juan García Hurtado, Villena
Federico Madrid, Alicante
Ricardo Madrid, Alicante
Hijo de Luis García Poveda, Villena
Salvador Poveda, Villena
Bodegas Schenk, Alicante

VALENCIA, UTIEL-REQUENA, AND CHESTE

C. Augusto Egli, S.L.
Vte. Gandía Pla

A. y J. Garrigos, S.L.
José Hernández Iranzo

Vicente Lambies Grancha
Bodegas Levantinas Españolas, S.A.
Ramón Mestre Serra
J. A. Mompo
Nuevas Industrias, S.A.
Antonio Pérez Calvo
Hijos de Pons Hermanos

Bodegas Schenk, S.A.
Francisco Selma Cerrillo
Ferd. Steiner, S.A.
Teschendorff y Cía
Ch. Valsangiacomo, S.A.
Vinícolas de Occidente

TARRAGONA

Amigó Hermanos y Cía, Reus
René Barbier y Cía, S.V., Tarragona
S. A. Byres, Tarragona
Bablo Casas Vidiella, Reus
Cochs, S.A., Reus
Dalmau Hermanos y Cía Sucesores, Tarragona
Amadeo Ferraté, Reus
Fernando Gerhard, Valls
José López Bertrán y Cía, Tarragona
José Mª Martí Roig, Reus
Ramón Mestre Serra, Reus
Emilio Miró Salvat, Reus
S.A.F. Miró Sans, Reus
Bodegas Montblanch, S.A., Tarragona
Juan Mory y Cía, S.A., Tarragona

De Muller, S.A., Tarragona
José Mª Pamies Torres, Tarragona
Vda. de Luís Quer, S.L., Reus
Vinos Ricart, S.A., Reus
Hijos de Marcelino Rofes, Reus
Bodegas Salvat, S.A., Reus
Francisco Simó y Cía, Reus
Ferd. Steiner, S.A., Tarragona
Bodegas Tapias, S.A., Tarragona
La Tarraco Vinícola, S.L., Tarragona
Juan Tous Grand, Reus
Antonio Valls Juliá, Gandesa
Vinos Ventosa, S.L., Tarragona
La Vinícola Ibérica, S.A., Tarragona
Vinícola Reusense, S.A., Reus
E. Yzaguirre, S.A., Reus

PRIORATO

Amigó Hermanos y Cía, Reus
René Barbier y Cía, S.V., Tarragona
S.A. Byres, Tarragona
Pablo Casas Vidiella, Reus
Dalmau Hermanos y Cía Sucesores, Tarragona
Amadeo Ferraté, Reus
José López Bertrán y Cía, Tarragona
Ramón Mestre Serra, Reus
Emilio Miró Salvat, Reus
S.A.F. Miró Sans, Reus
Bodegas Montblanch, S.A., Tarragona
Juan Mory y Cía, S.A., Tarragona

De Muller, S.A., Tarragona
José Mª Pamies Torres, Tarragona
Vda de Luís Quer, S.L., Reus
Vinos Ricart, S.A., Reus
Hijos de Marcelino Rofes, Reus
Bodegas Salvat, S.A., Reus
Francisco Simó y Cía, Reus
Ferd. Steiner, S.A., Tarragona
Bodegas Tapias, S.A., Tarragona
La Tarraco Vinícola, S.L., Tarragona
S.A. "La Vid", La Secuita
La Vinícola Ibérica, S.A., Tarragona
E. Yzaguirre, S.A., Reus

PANADES

Cavas Albertí, Villafranca del Panadés

José Alegret Sanromá, Villafranca del Panadés

Aquila Rossa, S.A., Villafranca del Panadés

Batlle y Montserrat, S.L., Monjos (Barcelona)

J. B. Berger, S.A., Villafranca del Panadés

Bodegas Bosch-Güell, S.A., Villafranca del Panadés

Codorníu, S.A., San Sadurní de Noya

José Freixedas y Cía, S.L., Villafranca del Panadés

José Freixedas Bové, Villafranca del Panadés

Freixenet, S.A., San Sadurní de Noya

J. Font, Castellví de la Marca (Barcelona)

Juan Güell Fábregas, Villafranca del Panadés

Cavas Hill, Moja (Barcelona)

Luis Marcé y Cía, S.L., Villafranca del Panadés

Narciso Mascaró Marcé, Villafranca del Panadés

Juan Montaner Muntané, Villafranca del Panadés

Domingo Montserrat, Villafranca del Panadés

Juan Mory y Cía, S.A., Villafranca del Panadés

Francisco Olivella, Villafranca del Panadés

Cavas Parés Baltá, S.A., Pachs del Panadés

Cavas Raventós Catasús, S.A., Villafranca del Panadés

Bodegas J. Robert, Sitges

Ginés Rovira, Villafranca del Panadés

Hermanos Segura Viudas, San Sadurní de Noya

José Mª Sogas Muntaner, Villafranca del Panadés

Juan Solé Montané, Villafranca del Panadés

José Mª Tetas Vendrell, Villafranca del Panadés

Miguel Torres Carbó, Villafranca del Panadés

Salvador Vallés Marrugat, Monjos (Barcelona)

HUELVA

D. Juan Camacho Acosta, Bollullos par del Condado

D. Miguel Salas Acosta, Bollullos par del Condado

D. Antonio Benjumea Román, Bollullos par del Condado

Dña Concepción Calero Calero, La Palma del Condado

Bodegas J. Calvo (José Calvo Cadaval), Bollullos par del Condado

D. Francisco Camacho Camacho, Bollullos par del Condado

D. Juan Camacho Camacho, Bollullos par del Condado

D. José Iglesias Carrellán, Bollullos par del Condado

D. Antonio Valdera Carrellán, Bollullos par del Condado

D. José Mª Castizo Pinto, La Palma del Condado

D. Antonio Clemente Robles, Bollullos par del Condado

D. Alfonso Daza Suárez, Chucena

D. Rafael Diaz Caparrós, Bollullos par del Condado

Hijos de Julian Espinosa, S.R.C., La Palma del Condado

D. Celedonio Ferrero Conca, Rociana del Condado

D. Gregorio García Pérez, Bollullos par del Condado

D. Agustin Genovés Barberá, La Palma del Condado

Casa Lazo, S.A., San Juan del Puerto

E. Flores Macias y Cía, Moguer

Srs José y Miguel Martín Alvárez, Bollullos per del Condado

Hijos de Carlos M. Morales, S.L., La Palma del Condado

D. Juan Oliveros Perea, Bollullos par del Condado

Bodegas Oro, S.L., Bollullos par del Condado

D. José Ortega Ligero, Rociana del Condado

D. Manuel Perea Diaz, Bollullos par del Condado

D. Pedro Pérez Clavijo, Bollullos par del Condado

Bodegas Pichardo, S.L., La Palma del Condado

Bodegas Ramos (D. Fco Ramos Mantis), Bollullos par del Condado

D. Rafael Salas López, La Palma del Condado

D. Manuel Galán Sánchez-Matamoros, Villalba del Alcor

D. José Sauci Diaz, Bollullos par del Condado

Bodegas Toro, S.R.C., La Palma del Condado

D. Alonso Valdayo Terriza, Bollullos par del Condado

Hijos de Francisco Vallejo, S.L., Bollullos par del Condado

D. Antonio Villarán Ramos, Bollullos par del Condado

ALLELA

Alella Vinícola

Jaime Serra Güell

CARIÑENA

Aragonesa Vinícola, S.A., Zaragoza
Balbino Lacosta Tello, Zaragoza
Bodega Cooperativa de San Valero, Cariñena

Francisco García Blasco, Zaragoza
Sucesores de Gerónimo Paricio, Zaragoza

EXPORTERS OF SHERRY FROM SPAIN
TO MEMBERS OF
THE SHERRY SHIPPERS ASSOCIATION

EXPORTER	BRAND	DESCRIPTION
Bertola, S.A.	'Amontillado "50"'	Dry: bottled in Spain
Jerez de la Frontera	'Bertola Brown'	Solera 1852; sweet, rich
	'Bertola Cream'	Pale old *oloroso*
	'Bertola Dry'	Light, dry *amontillado fino*
	'Bertola Fino Four'	Very dry
	'Bertola Medium'	*Amontillado*
	'Farandola'	Medium sweet
	'Jerez Oloroso'	Light golden
	'Manzanilla'	Light dry
	'Royal Amontillado'	
	'Royal Double'	*Oloroso*

Imported by Evans, Marshall & Co. Ltd, London

John William Burdon	'Curiously Dry'	Natural *fino*
Puerto de Santa María	'Don John'	*Manzanilla*
Sanlúcar de	'Heavenly Cream'	*Oloroso*
Barrameda		
Chipiona		

Imported by Coleman & Co. Ltd, Norwich

Luis Caballero, S.A.	'Gran Señor Choice Old	
Puerto de Santa María	Cream Sherry'	
	'Gran Señor Amontillado	
	Sherry'	

Imported by Wm & Jno Lockett (Wines & Spirits) Ltd, Liverpool

José de la Cuesta	'Cuesta Alondra'	Dry *fino*
Puerto de Santa María	'Cuesta Cara Mía'	Old East India Brown
	'Cuesta Don Luis'	Old dry
	'Cuesta Gallina'	*Manzanilla*

Plate 16. The Sherry town of Puerto de Santa
María: sun-drenched grapes are taken
to the treading-floor (*see* Chapter 2)
(By courtesy of Harvey's, Bristol)
Percy Hennell

EXPORTER	BRAND	DESCRIPTION
José de la Cuesta	'Cuesta Melisa'	*Oloroso*
Puerto de Santa María	'Cuesta Preferido'	Cream
	'Cuesta Queen'	*Amontillado*
	'Cuesta Vasco'	Pale

Imported by Charles Kinloch & Co. Ltd, London

Cuvillo y Cía	'Cuvillo Cream'	Very old *oloroso*; average age more than 50 years
Puerto de Santa María	'Fabuloso'	Old dry *oloroso*; average age more than 100 years
	'Fino C'	

Imported by Cuvillo & Co. (London) Ltd, London
(This company has shipped Sherry to Britain since its foundation in 1783, when it was known as M. M. de Mora)

Eduardo Delage	'London Cream'	*Oloroso*
Jerez de la Frontera	'London Dry'	*Fino*
	'London Milk'	Medium sweet *oloroso*

Imported by John Martin of London Ltd, London

Pedro Domecq, S.A.	'Autumn Brown'	Brown
Jerez de la Frontera	'Botaina'	*Amontillado*
	'Brown Beauty'	Brown
	'Casino'	*Amontillado*
	'Celebration Cream'	Cream *oloroso*
	'Double Century'	*Oloroso*
	'La Ina'	*Fino*

Imported by Luis Gordon & Son Ltd, London

Duff Gordon & Co.	'Bodega'	Pale dry, medium and cream
Puerto de Santa María	'Cream Sherry	*Oloroso*
	'El Cid'	*Amontillado*
	'Fino Feria'	Pale dry *fino*
	'Santa María'	Cream

Imported by Rutherford, Osborne & Perkin Ltd, London
(The house of Duff Gordon was founded in 1768 at Cádiz, moving to Puerto de Santa María in 1823)

EXPORTER	BRAND	DESCRIPTION
Manuel Fernández y Cía Ltda	'Affinity'	*Fino*
	'Fernandilla'	*Manzanilla*
Bobadilla y Cía Ltda	'Sadana'	*Amontillado*
Jerez de la Frontera	'Sareda'	Old Brown
	'Southern Cream'	Fine old *oloroso*

Imported by W. E. Smith & Co Ltd, London

R. D. Ferraro Jerez de la Frontera	'Taylor's Amontillado Sherry' 'Taylor's Cream Sherry' 'Taylor's Fino Dry Sherry' 'Taylor's Old Nut Brown Sherry'	

Imported by David Taylor & Son Ltd, London, whose 'Taylor's Cream Sherry' won the Prix D'Honneur at the Brussels 1963 Olympiades Mondiales Des Vins, Alcools, et Liqueurs; and the Gold Medal and Diploma in the London 1964 British Bottlers' Institute Sherry, Port, and Madeira Wine Competition

Flores Hermanos Puerta de Santa María	'Fandango' (Solera originally laid down in 1914)	⎰ *Oloroso* ⎱ Cream ⎰ *Amontillado* ⎱ *Fino*
	'Secosac'	Pale, dry, and nutty

Imported by Blumenthals Ltd, London

Florido Hermanos Sanlúcar de Barrameda	'Clásica'	*Manzanilla*
	'Cream of Andalucia'	Rich cream
	'Monopole'	*Oloroso*
	'Old Pardo'	Rich Brown
	'Selecto'	*Amontillado*

Imported by C. Buswell & Co. Ltd, London

Garvey, S.A. Jerez de la Frontera	'Flor de Jerez'	*Oloroso*
	'San Patricio'	*Fino*
	'Tío Guillermo'	Fine old *amontillado*, bottled in Spain

Imported by Percy Fox & Co. Ltd, London
(Garvey's, founded by an Irishman, was the first firm to export *fino* Sherry from Jerez, and 'San Patricio' was named after the founder's son Patrick)

EXPORTER	BRAND	DESCRIPTION
González Byass y Cía Jerez de la Frontera	'La Majestad'	⎧ *Amontillado* ⎨ Brown ⎩ Cream *Fino*
	'Tío Pepe'	Very dry *fino*

Imported by Blumenthals Ltd, London

Mackenzie y Cía Jerez de la Frontera	'El Catador'	Natural *fino*, very dry
	'Exquisito'	Old cream
	'Golden Glory'	Medium sweet *oloroso*
	'Manzanilla Fina'	Very dry
	'Pasa-Doble'	Old *amontillado*
	'Perla'	Medium
	'Rich Brown'	Dark sweet
	'Vintners Choice'	*Amontillado*, medium dry
	'Vintners Cream'	*Oloroso*, sweet

Imported by Mackenzie & Co. Ltd, London

José Martínez, S.L. Jerez de la Frontera	'Alegría'	*Manzanilla*
	'Amador'	*Amontillado*
	'Rayoso Cream'	*Oloroso*

Imported by Davis, Hammond & Barton Ltd, London

Martínez Gassiot (España) Ltda Jerez de la Frontera	'Copelia Cream'	*Oloroso*
	'Fino Basilio'	*Fino*
	'La Cazita'	Pale, dry
	'Madrigal'	*Oloroso*
	'Spanish Colours'	Full, pale

Imported by Martínez Gassiot & Co. Ltd, London

Miguel Mendoza y Cía Jerez de la Frontera	'Amontillado Gold Label'	
	'Dalucia'	*Amontillado*
	'La Fondaz'	Old cream
	'Sombrero'	⎧ Fine old nut brown ⎨ *Fino* ⎩ *Oloroso*

Unbranded pale and golden Sherry

Imported by Edward Young & Co. Ltd, London

EXPORTER	BRAND	DESCRIPTION
M. Misa, S.A. Jerez de la Frontera	'Abolengo'	*Amontillado* (bottled in Spain)
	'Fino Chiquilla'	Light *fino* (bottled in Spain)
	'La Novia'	Nutty *oloroso*
	'Manzanilla'	*Manzanilla*, light dry
	'Paladar'	Full *amontillado*
	'Romero'	Old *oloroso*

Imported by M. Misa, London

Palomino & Vergara, S.A. Jerez de la Frontera	'John Peter Amontillado'	
	'Marvilla Cream'	Medium and dry; slightly low strength
	'Palomino Oloroso'	
	'Palomino Pale Dry'	
	'Palomino Rich Golden'	
	'Palomino Spanish Cream'	
	'Palomino Vino de Pasto'	
	'Velvet Cream'	

Imported by Jules Duval & Beaufoys Ltd, Isleworth

José Ramírez & Co. Ltd Puerto de Santa María	'Amontillado fino'	
	'Cream'	
	'Lolita'	*Oloroso*
	'Manzanilla'	
	'Oloroso'	
	'Ramón'	Old rich brown

Imported by Southard & Co. Ltd, East Molesey
(The Ramírez family claim to be the oldest Sherry exporters in the Jerez district; the vineyards are planted on land granted to the family in 1495 after the reconquest of Granada from the Moors)

Herederos del Marqués del
  Real Tesoro, S.A.
  Jerez de la Frontera
	'Almirante'	*Oloroso*

	'Andaluz'	*Amoroso*
	'Ideal'	*Fino*
	'La Capitana'	*Manzanilla*
	'R.T. Fino'	Natural *fino* at natural Spanish strength; bottled in Spain
	'Torero'	*Amontillado*

EXPORTER	BRAND	DESCRIPTION
M. Antonio de la Riva, S.A. Jerez de la Frontera	'Amontillado La Riva'	Dry *amontillado*, but slightly sweetened for England
	'Carmela Cream'	
	'Doña Clara'	Old golden
	'Fino Hispano'	Light dry *fino*
	'Fino Tres Palmas'	Dry natural *fino* as drunk in Spain
	'Fortuna Manzanilla'	
	'Guadalupe Amontillado'	Natural Guadalupe as drunk in Spain
	'Macharnudo La Riva Fino'	Natural dry *fino*
	'Macharnudo La Riva Oloroso'	Natural *oloroso* as drunk in Spain
	'Royal La Riva Cream'	*Oloroso*, slightly sweetened
	'San José'	*Amontillado* medium dry
	'Viña La Riva Oloroso'	Very old natural *oloroso*, unsweetened
	'Viña Sabel'	*Oloroso* medium sweet

Imported by La Riva, London

J. M. Rivero Jerez de la Frontera	'C.Z.'	One dozen different types, including *fino*, *amontillado*, and *manzanilla*

Imported by John E. Fells & Son Ltd, London

Ruiz y Hermanos, A.R. Jerez de la Frontera	'Isabelita'	*Fino*

Imported by John Harvey & Sons Ltd, Bristol

Zoilo Ruiz-Mateos, S.A. Jerez de la Frontera	'Adorno'	*Amontillado*
	'Amoroso'	*Amontillado*, very old
	'Anita'	Brown, blended *oloroso*
	'Bank'	Old pale *amontillado*
	'Bristol Cream'	Old full pale
	'Bristol Dry'	Medium dry
	'Bristol Fino'	*Fino*
	'Bristol Milk'	Golden
	'Club Amontillado'	*Amontillado*

EXPORTER	BRAND	DESCRIPTION
Zoilo Ruiz-Mateos, S.A. Jerez de la Frontera	'Copper Beech'	Brown, blended *oloroso*
	'Crowsfoot'	*Oloroso*, very old
	'Falanda'	*Oloroso*
	'Fanfare'	Light golden *oloroso*
	'Fine Old Amontillado'	*Amontillado*
	'Golden'	*Oloroso*, very old
	'Luncheon Dry'	Light, pale *fino*
	'Manchita'	Light, medium dry *amontillado*
	'Manzanilla'	Light, pale, very dry
	'Margarita'	Medium dry *amontillado*
	'Merienda'	Medium *amontillado*
	'Montilla'	Old, very pale, dry *amontillado*
	'Oloroso Viejo'	*Oloroso*
	'Reina Victoria'	Dry, old *amontillado*
	'Select Shooting'	*Oloroso*

Imported by John Harvey & Sons Ltd, Bristol

Sandeman Hermanos Jerez de la Frontera	'Apitiv'	Extra dry *fino*
	'Armada Cream'	Fine old *oloroso*
	'Brown Sherry'	Fine, rich
	'De Luxe'	Fine rich *palo cortado*
	'Dry Don'	Medium dry *amontillado*
	'Pale Sherry'	Medium dry

Imported by Geo. G. Sandeman Sons & Co. Ltd, London

	'Amontillado'	
	'Fino'	
	'400'	Rich *oloroso*
	'Phillips Bristol Milk'	*Oloroso*
	'Rich Cream'	Blend of old wines

Imported by J. R. Phillips & Co. Ltd, London

Williams & Humbert, Ltd Jerez de la Frontera	'As You Like It'	Old *oloroso*, cream
	'A Winter's Tale'	Old, matured in cask
	'Carlito'	Pale *amontillado*
	'Cedro'	Medium dry
	'Dry Sack'	*Oloroso*
	'Equator'	Very old, almost completely dry

EXPORTER	BRAND	DESCRIPTION
Williams & Humbert, Ltd	'Molino'	Medium sweet *oloroso*
Jerez de la Frontera	'Old East India'	Rich brown
	'Pando'	Very dry *fino*
	'Walnut Brown'	

Imported by Williams & Humbert Ltd, London

Wilson & Valdespino	'Fino Inocente'	Macharnudo *fino*
Jerez de la Frontera	'Jerez Cream'	Old *oloroso*
	'Martial Amontillado'	
	'Martial Golden'	*Oloroso*
	'Montana Manzanilla'	Very dry
	'Tío Diego'	Dry *amontillado*

Imported by Wilson & Valdespino Ltd, London

SPANISH BRANDY EXPORTERS

EXPORTER	PLACE	BRAND	IMPORTER
Alvear, S.A.	Montilla		
Bertola, S.A.	Jerez de la Frontera		
Hijos de Agustín Blázquez	Cádiz	'Tonel Solo' 'Felipe II' 'Tres Medallas'	
John William Burdon	Puerto de Santa María	'Decano' 'Millenario'	
Luis Caballero, S.A.	Puerto de Santa María		
Eduardo Delage	Jerez de la Frontera		
Diez Hermanos	Jerez de la Frontera		
Pedro Domecq, S.A.	Jerez de la Frontera	'Three Vines' 'Fundador' 'Carlos I'	Luis Gordon & Sons Ltd, London
Duff Gordon & Co.	Puerto de Santa María		Rutherford, Osborne & Perkin Ltd, London
Manuel Fernández y Cía S.L.	Jerez de la Frontera		W. E. Smith & Co. Ltd, London
Garvey, S.A.	Jerez de la Frontera		
González Byass y Cía	Jerez de la Frontera	'Soberano' 'Lepanto'	
Alejandro Gordon	Jerez de la Frontera		
Manuel Guerrero y Cía	Jerez de la Frontera		
Hijos de Jiménez Varela	Puerto de Santa María		
Larios, S.A.	Málaga		
Emilio Lustau, S.A.	Jerez de la Frontera		
Marqués del Mérito, S.A.	Jerez de la Frontera		
Osborne y Cía, S.A.	Puerto de Santa María		
Herederos del Marqués del Real Tesoro, S.A.	Jerez de la Frontera	'Gladiator' 'Almirante'	
M. Antonio de la Riva, S.A.	Jerez de la Frontera	'Hispano Tres Estrellas' 'Hispano Viejo 1870'	La Riva, London

EXPORTER	PLACE	BRAND	IMPORTER
M. Antonio de la Riva, S.A.	Jerez de la Frontera	'San Quintin Solera Especial'	La Riva, London
Tomás Rivero y Hermanos, S.L.	Jerez de la Frontera		
Sánchez Romate Hermanos	Jerez de la Frontera		
Zoilo Ruiz-Mateos, S.A.	Jerez de la Frontera		
Félix Ruiz y Ruiz, S.L.	Jerez de la Frontera		
Sandeman Hermanos	Jerez de la Frontera	'Cape Negra'	Geo. G. Sandeman Sons & Co. Ltd, London
José de Soto, S.A.	Jerez de la Frontera		
Fernando A. de Terry, S.A.	Puerto de Santa María	'Terry 1' 'Solera 1900' 'Especial Terry' 'V.O.' 'Competidor' 'Centenario'	
A. R. Valdespino, S.A.	Jerez de la Frontera	'1850' 'Valdespino'	
Williams & Humbert Ltd	Jerez de la Frontera		

EXPORT OF WINES AND SPIRITS FROM SPAIN
IN 1964

AREAS OF ORIGIN	ORDINARY OR TABLE WINES	CHOICE WINES DRY	WINES SWEET	SPARKLING WINES	TOTAL: WINES.
	Litres	*Litres*	*Litres*	*Litres*	*Litres*
Alicante	16,888,544	—	22,082	—	16,910,626
Barcelona	3,547,370	36,455	1,246,320	467,610	5,297,755
Villafranca del Panadés	1,986,567	12,342	1,099,461	67,670	3,166,040
Ciudad Real	1,063,080	—	2,584	—	1,065,664
Córdoba	10,443	464,391	—	—	474,834
Guipúzcoa (Pasajes)	5,366,881	—	35,763	—	5,402,644
Huelva	359,800	42,043	6,211	—	408,054
Jerez de la Frontera	—	44,541,801	—	—	44,541,801
Logroño (Rioja)	21,469,886	—	—	13,134	21,483,020
Málaga	—	63,154	4,723,969	—	4,787,123
Navarre	3,283,093	—	—	3,400	3,286,493
Oviedo	—	—	—	—	—
Pontevedra	6,452	2,800	4,552	—	13,804
Santander	289,520	—	—	—	289,520
Segovia	—	—	—	—	—
Seville	51,631	711	695	—	53,037
Tarragona	—	17,665,283	16,363,001	955	34,029,239
Valencia	61,163,958	18,762,772	14,191,093	—	94,117,823
Valladolid	72	—	—	—	72
Vizcaya	544,780	—	—	—	544,780
Zaragoza	406,060	140,680	82,414	—	629,154
Total	116,438,137	81,732,432	37,778,145	552,769	236,501,483

AREAS OF ORIGIN	LIQUEURS	BRANDIES	TOTAL: SPIRITS	GRAND TOTAL: WINES AND SPIRITS	TOTAL ESTIMATED VALUE
	Litres	*Litres*	*Litres*	*Litres*	*Pesetas*
Alicante	—	—	—	16,910,626	77,470,406
Barcelona	769,306	27,136	796,442	6,094,197	102,493,737
Villafranca del Panadés	36,760	3,924	40,684	3,206,724	28,053,408
Ciudad Real	15,000	22,500	37,500	1,103,164	9,145,139
Córdoba	5,506	7,143	12,649	487,483	9,939,528
Guipúzcoa (Pasajes)	465	—	465	5,403,109	24,097,289
Huelva	1,312	1,440	2,752	410,806	2,813,220
Jerez de la Frontera	—	10,422,181	10,422,181	54,963,982	1,981,461,839
Logroño (Rioja)	135	—	135	21,483,155	206,178,988
Málaga	16,492	7,168	23,660	4,810,783	38,727,865
Navarre	2,677	—	2,677	3,289,170	14,417,094
Oviedo	9,132	450	9,582	9,582	515,494
Pontevedra	360	—	360	14,164	533,494
Santander	1,440	12,600	14,040	303,560	2,418,595
Segovia	64,286	—	64,286	64,286	3,644,205
Seville	—	—	—	53,037	772,555
Tarragona	88,078	—	88,078	34,117,317	237,947,468
Valencia	6,308	16,472	22,780	94,140,603	442,377,506
Valladolid	—	—	—	72	14,220
Vizcaya	—	—	—	544,780	6,999,814
Zaragoza	—	—	—	629,154	2,816,309
Total	1,017,257	10,521,014	11,538,271	248,039,754	3,192,838,173

APPROXIMATE ACREAGE OF SPANISH VINEYARDS AND QUANTITIES OF WINE PRODUCED*

		Acres (approx.)	Gallons (average)
CENTRAL SPAIN			
Castile		1,440,000	168,416,000
Aragon		320,000	21,972,000
León		307,000	23,759,000
Extremadura		194,000	26,962,000
	Totals	2,261,000	241,109,000
MEDITERRANEAN			
Levante		810,000	58,441,000
Catalonia and			
Balearic Isles		500,000	92,922,000
Andalusia		282,000	31,445,000
	Totals	1,592,000	182,808,000
ATLANTIC			
Rioja		187,000	40,301,000
Galicia		94,000	43,542,000
Basque Provinces		14,000	3,663,000
Asturias		4,000	708,000
Canaries		20,000	635,000
	Totals	319,000	88,849,000
	Grand Totals	4,172,000	512,766,000

* Extracted, with his kind permission, from André L. Simon's *The Commonsense of Wine*.

CAPACITIES OF SPANISH WINE-CONTAINERS

As the sizes of wine-containers vary slightly from one bodega to another, the figures given below are approximate.

1 gallon = 4·546 litres

JEREZ
Double butt	225 gallons
Bodega butt	132–146 gallons
Bocoy	146½ gallons
Bota de recibo	112 gallons
Shipping butt	108 gallons
Hogshead	54 gallons
Quarter-cask	27 gallons
Octave	13½ gallons
English bottle	1⅓ pints
Spanish bottle	1¼ pints

RIOJA
Cuba	4,400 gallons
Tino	1,760 or 2,200 gallons
Bocoy	132 gallons
Barrica bordelesa	48 gallons
Cuarterola (quarter-cask)	22 gallons
Cántara	3½ gallons
Comporta	220–220 pounds (grapes)

VALDEPEÑAS
Bocoy	176 gallons
Cuba	54 gallons
Barrica	49½ gallons
Arroba	3½ gallons

MALAGA
Arroba	3½ gallons

TARRAGONA
Drum	145 gallons
Pipe	115 gallons
Half-drum	88 gallons

PANADÉS AND PRIORATO
Bombona	6½ gallons

GLOSSARY OF SPANISH WORDS
AS USED IN THE TEXT

n., noun.　　*a.*, adjective.

albariza, *n.* White, chalky vineyard soil.

alpargata de
esparto Sandal made from esparto grass.

amontillado, *n.* Pale, dry Sherry with a mellow flavour.

amoroso, *n.* Golden, rich dessert Sherry.

arena, *n.* Sandy vineyard soil.

arroba, *n.* Liquid measure.

atroje, *n.* Large, slatted wooden cage in which grapes are pressed by their own weight.

barrica, *n.* Small keg, barrel.

barro, *n.* Mud, clay.

blanco, *a.* White.

bocoy, *n.* Hogshead.

bodega, *n.* Wine-cellar, warehouse, bar.

bombona, *n.* Pear-shaped glass jar for outdoor maturing of wine.

bota, *n.* Barrel, butt, leather wine-bottle.

camión, *n.* Van, lorry.

capataz, *n.* Head cellarman.

cava, *n.* Wine-cellar. (Applies to sparkling wines only.)

cementerio, *n.* 'Cemetery': private cellar.

comporta, *n.* Upright wooden container in which grapes are carried from the vineyard.

coñac, *n.* Brandy.

copita, *n.* Small glass with short stem and elongated bowl.

corriente, *a.* Everyday, ordinary.

cortado, *n.* Sherry classification: rich, nutty type.

criadera, *n.* 'Nursery' solera.

crianza, *n.* 'Breeding': maturation of wine.

denominación
de origen Controlled name of area of origin.

dulce, *a.* Sweet.

entremeses, *n.* Introductory dish.

estancia, *n.* Residence.

fino, *a.* 'Fine': light, dry, pale Sherry, delicate to taste.

flor, *n.* 'Flower', yeasty mould produced by fermentation.

garrafa, *n.* Decanter, carafe.

lagar, *n.* Wine-press.

manzanilla, *n.* Pale, dry Sherry with tart flavour; the word means 'small apple'.

mesa, *n.* Table (thus *vino de mesa* is 'table wine').

mistela, *n.* Very sweet grape-juice whose fermentation has been stopped at an early stage.

mosto, *n.* Must; grape-juice before it is fermented.

oloroso, *a.*	'Fragrant': full-bodied, golden to dark, rather sweet Sherry.
orujo, *n.*	Refuse from pressed grapes.
palma, *n.*	Sherry classification: fine and dry.
pellejo, *n.*	Wine-skin.
pisador, *n.*	Treader (of grapes).
ponche, *n.*	Punch.
porrón, *n.*	Wine-container with long spout.
portador, *n.*	'Porter': oval wooden container in which grapes are carried from the vineyard.
raya, *n.*	Sherry classification: usually *oloroso*.
rosado, *a.*	Rosé.
seco, *a.*	Dry.
solera, *n.*	Blend, vatting (of strong, old wine).
tinaja, *n.*	Large earthenware jar.
tinto, *a.*	Red.
vendimia, *n.*	Vintage.
venencia, *n.*	A long stick of sprung whalebone with a silver cup at one end and a hook at the other; used for tasting out of the butt.
viejo, *a.*	Old.
vino, *n.*	Wine.
zapato, *n.*	'Shoe': a special nail-studded shoe worn for treading grapes.

GLOSSARY OF FRENCH WORDS
AS USED IN THE TEXT

n., noun.   *a.*, adjective.

appellation contrôlée	Registered trade name of place of origin.
blanc de blanc, *a*	Made from white grapes only (describing Champagne).
brut, *a*	Unsweetened (describing Champagne).
cave, *n.*	Wine-cellar.
chais, *n.*	Place, above ground, for storing wine.
chaptalisation, *n.*	Addition of sugar to grape-juice before fermentation to increase the production of alcohol.
coupage, *n.*	Blending.
dégorgement, *n.*	Removal of sediment from a Champagne bottle by drawing the first cork after the neck of the bottle has been frozen.
eau-de-vie, *n.*	Distilled wine; a type of brandy.
liqueur, *n.*	Syrup used for sweetening Champagne.
maderisé, *a.*	Characteristic of old wine tasting and smelling rather like Maderia.
marc, *n.*	Brandy made from the skins and pips of pressed grapes.
marque, *n.*	Brand name.
méthode champenoise	Best method of making sparkling wine: the second fermentation is produced in the bottle, as when making Champagne.
méthode cuvée close	Method of making sparkling wine: the second fermentation is produced in bulk.
pétillant, *a.*	Slightly sparkling.
vigneron, *n.*	Wine-grower.

CONCISE BIBLIOGRAPHY

ALLEN, H. Warner. *A History of Wine*. London, Faber, 1961.

ALLEN, H. Warner. *Sherry and Port*. London, Constable, 1952.

ALLEN, H. Warner. *The Wines of Portugal*. London, Michael Joseph, 1963. New York, McGraw-Hill,1964.

CARLING, T. E. *Wine Aristocracy: A Guide to the Best Wines of the World*. London, Rockliff, 1957.

CROFT-COOKE, Rupert. *Sherry*. London, Putnam, 1955.

GROSSMAN, H. J. *Grossman's Guide to Wines, Spirits and Beers*. Revised edition. New York, Scribner, 1955.

HEALY, M. *Stay Me With Flagons: A Book about Wine*. London, Michael Joseph, 1963.

HORNIKEL, E. *The Great Wines of Europe*. London, Weidenfeld & Nicolson, 1965.

HYAMS, E. *Dionysus: A Social History of the Wine Vine*. London, Thames & Hudson, 1965.

JAMES, W. *A Word Book of Wine*. London, Dent, 1962.

JEFFS, Julian. *Sherry*. London, Faber, 1961.

LAYTON, T. A. *Modern Wines*. London, Heinemann, 1964.

LICHINE, A. *The Wines of France*. London, Cassell, 1964.

POSTGATE, Raymond. *The Plain Man's Guide to Wine*. London, Michael Joseph, 1965.

RAINBIRD, George. *A Pocket Book of Wine*. London, Evans Brothers, 1963.

RAY, Cyril. *The Complete Imbiber*. Nos. 1–4, London, Putnam, 1956–60. Nos. 5, 6, London, Vista, 1963; No. 7, 1964.

SHAND, P. Morton. *A Book of French Wine*. Revised edition. London, Cape, 1960.

SHAND, P. Morton. *A Book of Wine*. London, Guy Chapman, 1926.

SIMON, André L. *The Commonsense of Wine*. London, Wine & Food Society, 1966.

SIMON, André L. *Know Your Wines*. London, Newman Neame, 1956.

SIMON, André L. *The Noble Grapes and the Great Wines of France*. London and New York, McGraw-Hill, 1957.

SIMON, André L., and HALLGARTEN, S. F. *The Great Wines of Germany and Its Famed Vineyards*. London and New York, McGraw-Hill, 1963.

WAUGH, A. *In Praise of Wine*. London, Cassell, 1959.

YOUNGER, William. *Gods, Men and Wine*. London, Wine & Food Society, 1966.

INDEX

References in **bold** type are to the pages on which the illustrations appear.

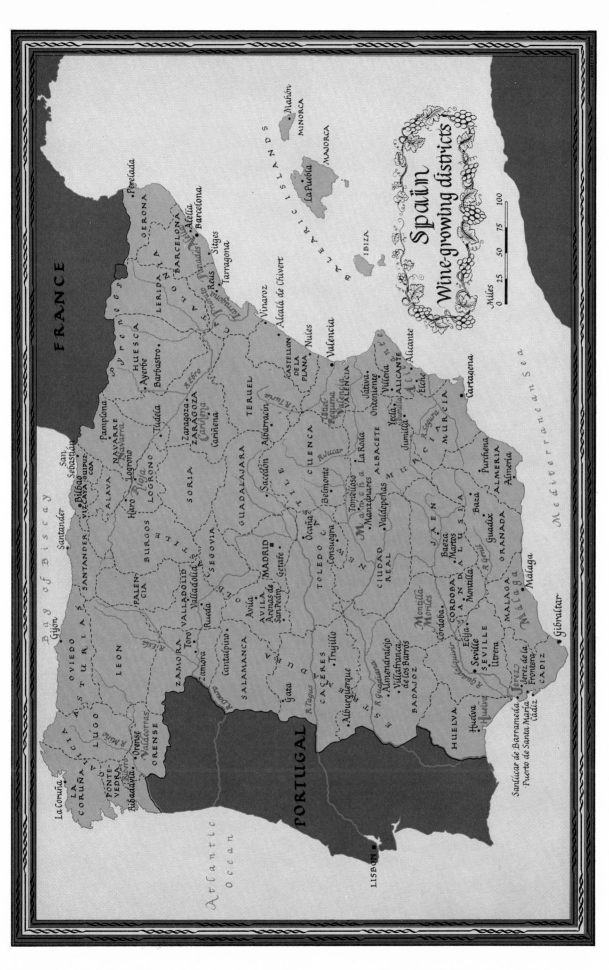

Spain
Wine-growing districts

Miles
0   25   50   75   100

FRANCE

PORTUGAL

Atlantic Ocean

Bay of Biscay

Mediterranean Sea

BALEARIC ISLANDS

MINORCA
Mahón
MAJORCA
La Puebla
IBIZA

LISBON

La Coruña
LA CORUÑA
PONTE-VEDRA
Ribadavia
Orense
ORENSE
VALDEORRAS
LUGO
Gijón
OVIEDO
ASTURIAS
Santander
SANTANDER
San Sebastián
GUIPUZ-COA
VIZCAYA
Bilbao
ALAVA
Pamplona
NAVARRE
Logroño
LOGROÑO
Rioja
Haro
BURGOS
SORIA
GUADALAJARA
Tudela
Zaragoza
ZARAGOZA
Carineña
Cariñena
HUESCA
Ayerbe
Barbastro
Pereleda
GERONA
LERIDA
BARCELONA
Acella
Barcelona
Sitges
Reus
Tarragona
Pyrenees
R. Ebro
TERUEL
Albarracín
CUENCA
Belmonte
Sacedón
R. Júcar
CASTELLON DE LA PLANA
Vinaroz
Alcalá de Chivert
Nules
Valencia
VALENCIA
Requena
Utiel
Ontenlente
Játiva
Villena
Alicante
ALICANTE
Elche
Cartagena
MURCIA
Jumilla
Yecla
ALMERIA
Almería
Purchena
Baza
GRANADA
Guadix
R. Genil
MALAGA
Málaga
Gibraltar
Montilla Moriles
Montilla
CORDOBA
Córdoba
Écija
SEVILLE
Seville
Utrera
ANDALUSIA
JAEN
Baeza
Martos
R. Guadalquivir
CADIZ
Jerez de la Frontera
Cádiz
Puerto de Santa María
Sanlúcar de Barrameda
HUELVA
Huelva
R. Odiel
BADAJOZ
Villafranca de los Barros
Almendralejo
Alburquerque
CACERES
Trujillo
Gata
R. Guadiana
R. Tagus
TOLEDO
Ocaña
Consuegra
CIUDAD REAL
Valdepeñas
Manzanares
Tomelloso
La Roda
ALBACETE
Mancha
MADRID
Getafe
SEGOVIA
AVILA
Avila
Arenas de San Pedro
VALLADOLID
Valladolid
Rueda
R. Duero
RIOSECO
Toro
ZAMORA
Zamora
Cantalpino
SALAMANCA
LEON
GALICIA
R. Miño
R. Sil
R. Turia
R. Segura
R. Almanzora
R. Gata
Ace.
MURCIA

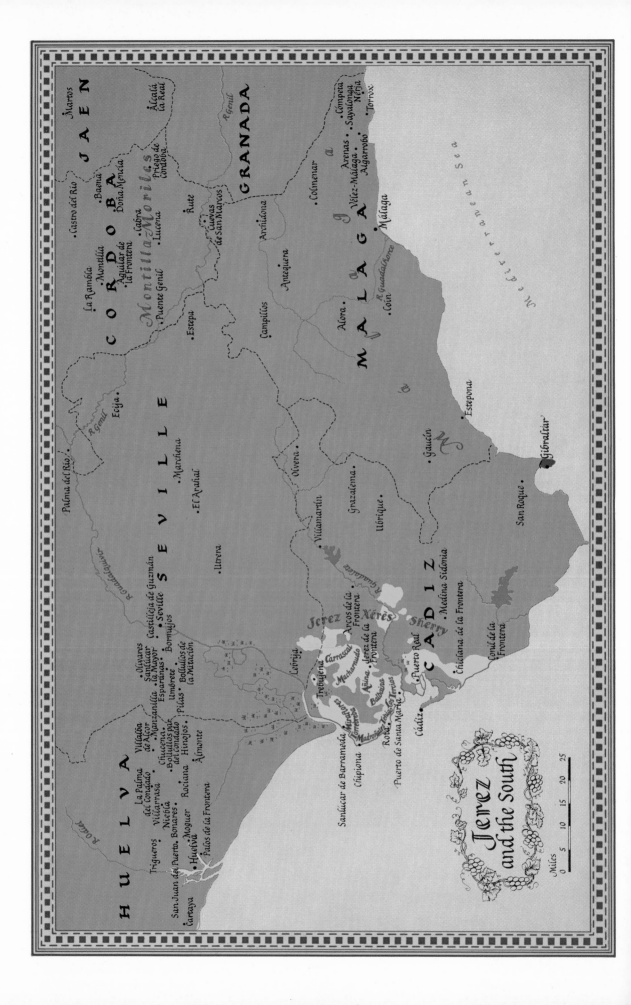

Jerez and the South

Miles

0 5 10 15 20 25

HUELVA

Rosal

Cartaya
San Juan del Puerto, Bonares
Trigueros
Huelva
Moguer
Rociana
Palos de la Frontera
Ayamonte
Villarrasa
Niebla
La Palma del Condado
Villalba de Alcor
Chucena
Bollullos par del Condado
Hinojos

SEVILLE

Palma del Río.
R. genil
Ecija.
R. Guadalquivir
Olivares
Sanlúcar la Mayor
Castilleja de Guzmán
Seville
Bormujos
Espartinas
Umbrete
Pilas
Bollullos de la Mitación
El Arahal
Marchena
Illora

CÓRDOBA

Castro del Río.
Baena.
Doña-Mencía
La Rambla
Montilla
Aguilar de la Frontera
Montilla-Moriles
Cabra
Lucena
Puente genil
Rute
Cuevas de San Marcos

JAEN

Martos
Alcalá la Real
Priego de Córdoba

GRANADA

R. genil
Estepa
Campillos
Antequera
Archidona

MALAGA

Colmenar
Competa
Arenas
Sayalonga
Nerja
Torrox
Vélez-Málaga
Algarrobo
Málaga
R. Guadalhorce
Coín
Alora
Gaucín
Estepona
San Roque
Gibraltar

CADIZ

Villamartín
Olvera
Grazalema
Ubrique
Arcos de la Frontera
Medina Sidonia
Jerez de la Frontera
Puerto Real
Conil de la Frontera
Chiclana de la Frontera
Cádiz
Puerto de Santa María
Rota
Chipiona
Sanlúcar de Barrameda
Lebrija
Trebujena
Carrascal
Machernudo
Añina
Balbaína
Los Tercios
Torrox
Madroñete
Corchuelo
Miraflores

Jerez
Xérès
Sherry

R. Guadalete

Mediterranean sea

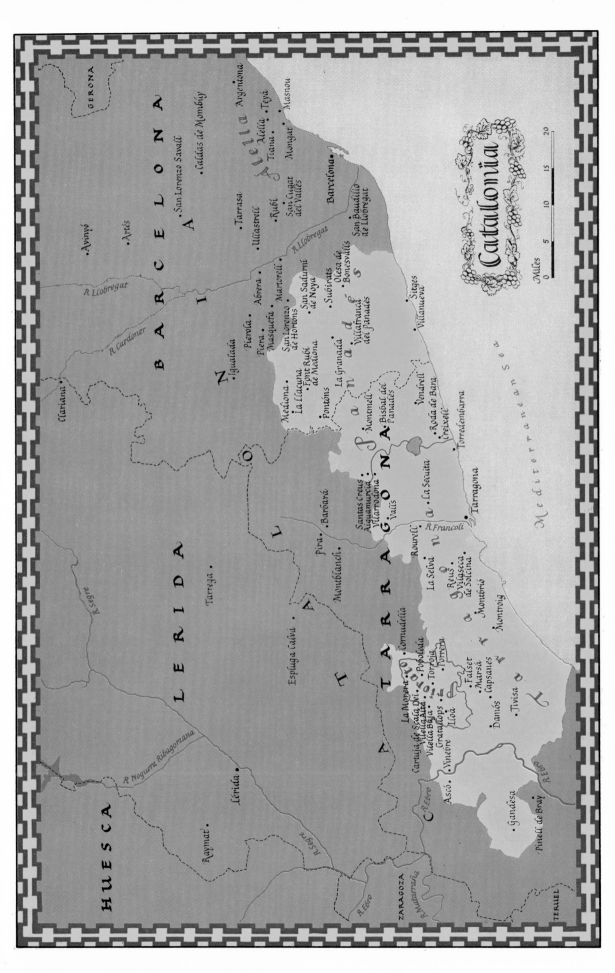

HUESCA

GERONA

BARCELONA

Avinyó

Artés

San Lorenzo Savall

Galáss de Mombuy

Argentona

Alella

Tiana • Teyá

Alella

Masnou

Tarrasa

Ullastrell

Rubí

San Cugat del Vallés

Mongat

Barcelona

San Baudilio de Llobregat

R. Llobregat

R. Llobregat

R. Cardoner

Cariana

Pierola

Fieu

Masquefa

Martorell

Abrera

San Lorenzo de Horrons

Font Rubí de Medona

Olesa de Bonesvalls

Suñirats

San Sadurní de Noya

Villafranca del Panadés

La Granada

Sitges

Vendrell

Villanueva

Igualada

N

Medona

La Llacuna

Pontons

Montmell

Bisbal del Panadés

Roda de Bará

Creixell

Torredembarra

O

Santas Creus

Aiguamurcia

Vilarrodona

Pera

Barbará

Valls

La Secuita

Tarragona

Mediterranean Sea

L

Montblanch

Rourell

R. Francoli

LERIDA

Tarrega

Espluga Cabra

La Selva

Reus

Vilaseca de Solcina

Montbrió

Montroig

TARRAGONA

R. Segre

Cornudella

Pobolxda

Porrera

Falset

Marsá

Capsanes

Tivisa

La Morera

Scala Dei

Vilella Alta

Cartuja de Scala Dei

Gratallops

Vilella Baja

Lloá

Vinebre

Damós

R. Noguera Ribagorzana

Raymat

Lerida

Ascó

Masturranu

R. Ebro

Gandesa

Pinell de Bray

R. Ebro

R. Ebro

R. Segre

ZARAGOZA

TERUEL

Catalonia

Miles

0   5   10   15   20

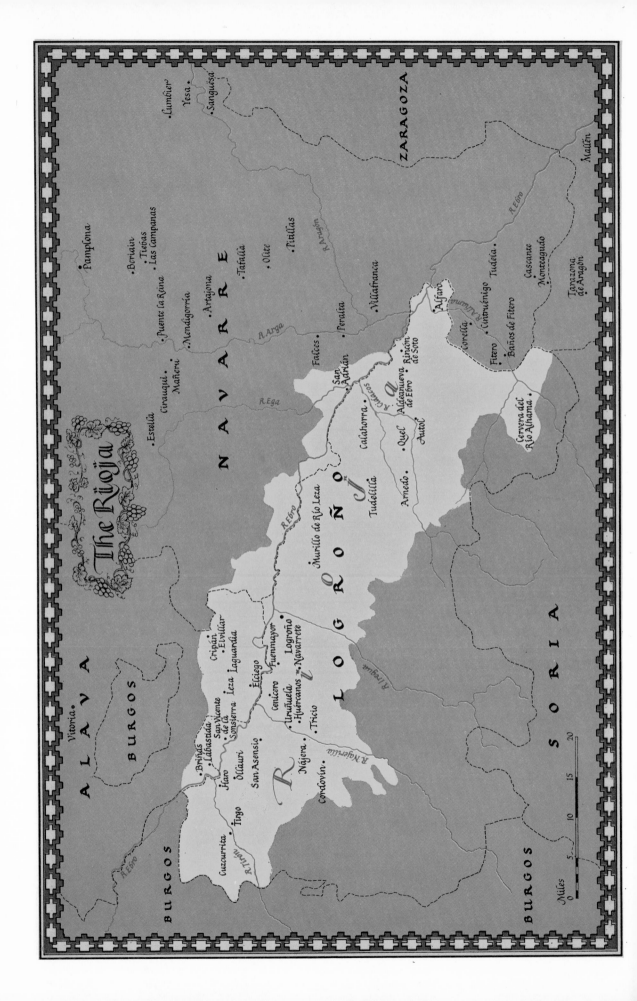

The Rioja